CULTURES OF THE WORLD

Uruguay

BALDWIN PUBLIC LIBRARY

Leslie Jermyn & Winnie Wong

Marshall Cavendish
Benchmark
New York

PICTURE CREDITS

Cover: © Galopin/Alamy
Alberto Baccaro/AFP/Getty Images: 29 • Ali Burafi/AFP/Getty Images: 38 • Audrius Tomonis: 135 • Bob Thomas/Popperfoto/Getty Images: 108 • Chip & Rosa Maria Peterson: 55, 61, 100 • Daniel Caselli/AFP/Getty Images: 8, 10, 43 • Daniel Garcia/AFP/Getty Images: 50 • Dante Fernandez/Latin Content/Getty Images: 119 • Dave G. Houser/Houserstock: 54, 59 • David Simson: 28, 53, 58, 74, 86, 102, 107 • Focus Team—Italy: 117, 118 • G. Richardson/Robert Harding World Imagery/Getty Images: 22 • Hart Preston/Time Life Pictures/Getty Images: 24 • Jan Butchofsky-Houser/Houserstock: 23, 52 • Krzysztof Dydynski/Lonely Planet Images: 2, 7, 63, 94, 122, 129 • Luis Marden/National Geographic Image Collection: 16 • Margie Politzer/Lonely Planet Images: 13, 72, 85, 114, 123 • Marty Melville/Getty Images: 39 • Michael Coyne/Lonely Planet Images: 64, 84, 97, 124, 126, 127 • Miguel Rojo/AFP/Getty Images: 20, 26, 30, 31, 71, 79, 91 • O. Louis Mazzatenta/National Geographic Image Collection: 44, 46, 49, 65, 66 • Pablo Porciuncula/AFP/Getty Images: 37 • Panta Astiazaran/AFP/Getty Images: 78, 80 • photolibrary: 1, 6, 11, 14, 32, 34, 40, 41, 48, 51, 56, 62, 76, 77, 96, 98, 105, 106, 113, 115, 131 • Robert Warren/Getty Images: 5, 68 • Tim Graham/Getty Images: 70 • Topham Picturepoint: 9, 67 • Wayne Walton/Lonely Planet Images: 111 • Win Initiative/Getty Images: 60, 82 • Win Initiative/The Image Bank/Getty Images: 69

PRECEDING PAGE

A man drinking maté from a gourd.

Publisher (U.S.): Michelle Bisson
Editors: Deborah Grahame, Stephanie Pee
Copyreader: Daphne Hougham
Designer: Benson Tan
Cover picture researcher: Connie Gardner
Picture researcher: Thomas Khoo

Marshall Cavendish Benchmark
99 White Plains Road
Tarrytown, NY 10591
Website: www.marshallcavendish.us

© Times Media Private Limited 1997
© Marshall Cavendish International (Asia) Private Limited 2010
® "Cultures of the World" is a registered trademark of Times Publishing Limited.

Originated and designed by Marshall Cavendish International (Asia) Private Limited
A member of Times Publishing Limited

Marshall Cavendish is a trademark of Times Publishing Limited.

Library of Congress Cataloging-in-Publication Data
Jermyn, Leslie.
   Uruguay / by Leslie Jermyn and Winnie Wong. — 2nd ed.
      p. cm. — (Cultures of the world)
   Summary: "Provides comprehensive information on the geography, history, wildlife, governmental structure, economy, cultural diversity, peoples, religion, and culture of Uruguay"—Provided by publisher.
   Includes bibliographical references and index.
   ISBN 978-0-7614-4482-4
   1. Uruguay—Juvenile literature. I. Wong, Winnie. II. Title.
   F2708.5.J47 2010
   989.5—dc22   2009007127

Printed in China
7 6 5 4 3 2 1

CONTENTS

INTRODUCTION

URUGUAY IS A SMALL COUNTRY **when measured by population** and landmass. It is shaped like an inverted diamond nestled between its two giant neighbors, Argentina and Brazil. Uruguay is famous for its livestock, agriculture, and football. The country has long supported advanced education, social security systems, and liberal laws. Both the Portuguese and the Spaniards have left their marks on this cosmopolitan country of many successive European migrations. Although it has had its share of attempted coups and military heavy-handedness, Uruguay has kept steadily moving forward. Since the return to civilian rule in 1985 after 12 painful years of military dictatorship, Uruguayans have taken very big steps in education, business, and tourism.

The traditional Uruguayan image of rugged independence and individualism is the manly gaucho, or cowboy livestock herder of the pampas, symbolizing the Uruguayans' pride in being, in their opinion, the most culturally advanced and egalitarian country in South America.

GEOGRAPHY

Santa Teresa Park, Uruguay

URUGUAY, OFFICIALLY REPÚBLICA Oriental del Uruguay, is a small country on the Atlantic seaboard of South America. Uruguay, located in southeastern South America, is sandwiched between the two largest countries of that continent: Brazil to the north and Argentina to the west.

Uruguay covers an area of about 68,000 square miles (176,120 square kilometers), slightly smaller than the U.S. state of Washington. The capital city, Montevideo, is in the south of the country on the Río de la Plata (Silver River).

The rocky coastline of Cabo Polonio Forest Park.

Uruguay is generally flatlands and rolling plains. It is watered by the Río de la Plata and the Río Uruguay. Most of the nation's agricultural activities take place around these rivers due to the rich alluvial soil found there. Uruguay enjoys a moderate, temperate climate. It is home to many different species of flora and fauna, but these are threatened by habitat loss.

The Río Cebollati in eastern Uruguay flows into the Merín Lagoon.

The perimeter of Uruguay is 1,024 miles (1,648 km) long, including a coastline of 410 miles (660 km). To the south is the Río de la Plata estuary where the Río Uruguay empties into the Atlantic Ocean. The Río Uruguay separates Uruguay from Argentina on the west, and the Merín Lagoon marks the border with Brazil in the northeast. In the north, Uruguay and Brazil are separated by the Río Cuareim. The most important river is the Río Negro, or Black River, which flows from northeast to southwest across the country.

URUGUAY'S REGIONS

Uruguay is made up of gently rolling grass-covered plains with no hills over 1,686 feet (514 m) above sea level. Two ridges of hills in the north and east of the country, called Cuchilla de Haedo and Cuchilla Grande, are where Monte Catedral, the country's highest point, can be found. Although there are no dramatic differences in geography across the country, there are three regions that differ noticeably in human settlement patterns and land use: the interior to the north, the Atlantic seaboard to the east, and the littoral, or shore, of the Río de la Plata and the Río Uruguay to the south and west.

THE INTERIOR This is the largest region, and it includes most of the central portion of the nation. It is mainly grassland with very little forest. Only 8.6 percent of the country is forested. These wooded areas, called gallery forests, grow along the edges of rivers. The soil of such an area is not very rich and therefore will not support intensive agriculture. Most of this land is used for raising cattle and sheep on large ranches.

THE ATLANTIC SEABOARD This is the band of land that stretches east from Montevideo in the south and then moves north toward Brazil along the Atlantic Ocean. Close to Montevideo the coastline is sandy and dotted with vacation resorts and small settlements of people who commute to Montevideo to

Playa Mansa (Mansa Beach) at Punta del Este, a favorite vacation destination of Uruguayans.

A rice field being harvested in José Pedro Varela.

work. The shore turns north at Punta del Este, or East Point—the biggest vacation resort in Uruguay.

THE LITTORAL This area consists of the shores of the Río de la Plata and the Río Uruguay to the west and north of Montevideo. Most of Uruguay's food crops are grown in this area. A bridge across the Uruguay River at Paysandú makes trade with Argentina very easy. Most Uruguayans live in this region—in Montevideo (population 1,347,888), Paysandú (115,222), and Salto (99,072). The greater Montevideo area, including Canelones and San José departments, is home to more than half of Uruguay's 3.5 million inhabitants.

The alluvial soil of the littoral, which is enriched by the periodic flooding of rivers, is the country's most arable land.

CLIMATE

Uruguay lies completely within the temperate zone, so the climate is moderate, with few extremes. There are four distinct seasons, but because

Uruguay is south of the equator, the seasons are the reverse of those in North America. January is the middle of summer with temperatures ranging from 70°F to 82°F (21°C to 28°C). July, the depth of winter, has average temperatures of 50°F to 61°F (10°C to 16°C). There is no distinct rainy season, though there is slightly more rainfall in the winter. Since there are no mountains, rain falls fairly evenly across the country. Rainfall averages 36 inches (91 cm) yearly. Winter and spring are characterized by high winds that are subject to rapid shifts in direction. With no natural barriers to stop them, winds can be violent, and sometimes tornadoes develop. Occasionally, cold north winds from the plains of Argentina cause temperatures to plunge in the winter, while winds off the Atlantic Ocean in the summer bring cooler temperatures.

FLORA AND FAUNA

Uruguay has the smallest forested area of all the South American countries. Besides its gallery forests—forests that form a strip along a river or wetland—that run for 466 miles (750 km) along the Uruguay River, tall prairie grass dominates the Uruguayan landscape.

The *Escallonia bifida*, an evergreen shrub in found in Uruguay, has small white flowers.

The fossilized skull of a giant capybara (a rodent), which measures 20.86 inches (53 cm) in diameter, was found stored in Uruguay's National History and Anthropology Museum by Andrés Rinderknecht and Ernesto Blanco, scientists from Montevideo. According to them, the rodent must have weighed 2,200 pounds (1,000 km)—bull-size. The small teeth suggest it fed mainly on vegetables and fruit.

The gallery forests contain a variety of trees—hardwoods such as *algarobo* (carob), *guayabo* (guava), quebracho (sumac), and *urunday*. One of the strangest trees in the country is the ombu, the bark of which appears soft and fluffy. Each ombu has its own unique shape. Its thick, twisting roots spread out over the ground. Some are over 500 years old and can be 6 feet (2 m) in diameter. The ceibo tree (*Erythrina crista-galli*, not to be confused with the cieba tree) has beautiful scarlet flowers. Palm trees grow along the southern shore. The rest of the country is covered with grasses and shrubs.

With so much water, both salt and fresh, there is an abundance of aquatic life. Freshwater fish include piranha, golden salmon, and pejerrey. *Pacú*, *tararira*, and *surubí* are similar to North American perch and bass. The Río de la Plata estuary is extremely rich in fauna. The fresh river water mingles with the warm ocean currents from Brazil and the colder ones from Argentina, giving the tidal estuary a mixture of fresh and salt waters. Sharks, rays, anchovies, and corvinas can be found in these waters.

The forests along the river and the lagoon marshes are home to dozens of species of birds. Some of the birds that live in wetlands are the royal duck, black-necked swan, creole duck, and various types of wild geese. The grasslands support partridges and the rhea (resembles a smaller ostrich).

Many of Uruguay's original larger mammals, such as the jaguar, puma, collared peccary, and giant anteater, are no longer found there because of loss of habitat and overhunting. Among those that remain are the foxes, white-lipped peccaries, armadillos, capybaras (*carpinchos*), coatimundis (type of raccoon), and three-toed anteaters. The Atlantic coast attracts a large colony of sea lions. They breed on Isla de Lobos, an island near Montevideo, and along the rocky eastern shore.

CITIES

MONTEVIDEO The biggest and most important city is Montevideo, the capital of Uruguay. Montevideo, with a population of approximately 1.4 million, is home to nearly half of all the people in Uruguay, making it almost a city-state. It is located across the Río de la Plata from Buenos Aires, Argentina. Six of Uruguay's universities are in Montevideo, as are most of its television,

WONDROUS ANIMALS OF URUGUAY

THE CAPYBARA *is the world's largest rodent. It usually lives near water, and its eyes and ears are positioned very high on its head to allow it to swim easily. Its partially webbed feet also help with swimming. This animal is hunted extensively for its meat in many parts of South America today.*

THE ARMADILLO *is one of the very few mammals that has a protective shell. Its shell is made up of strips of hard material called scutes that are bound together by flesh. When threatened, the armadillo will roll up in a ball to protect its soft underbelly. It also digs very fast and sometimes can dig its way to safety. W. H. Hudson, an English traveler to Uruguay in the 19th century, described the armadillo as a "little old bent-backed gentleman in a rusty black coat trotting briskly about on some very important business." Female armadillos give birth to identical litters of males or females, like genetic clones.*

THE *TAMANDUÁ*, OR THREE-TOED ANTEATER, *is a smaller cousin of the giant anteater, which is now extinct in Uruguay. The tamanduá spends about half its life in trees and is a very good climber. It has a prehensile tail that can grab and hold on to things like tree branches. Anteaters have large claws on their forefeet for self-defense and for breaking into insects' hiding places. They eat only insects but have no teeth to chew them with, so their hardy stomachs grind up the tough outer shells of insects like food processors.*

THE RHEA OR *ÑANDÚ* *is a large ostrichlike bird that stands 5 feet (1.5 m) tall and weighs about 50 pounds (23 k). It cannot fly but is a very speedy runner. Rheas live in family groups of one male and many females. All the females will lay their eggs in one nest for the male to incubate. These birds have long been hunted for their hides and feathers, which are used as dusters.*

Montevideo, the capital city of Uruguay, has a cosmopolitan heritage.

Deep beneath a great part of Uruguay is the famous underground Acuífero Guarani, one of the biggest freshwater reservoirs in the world. It stretches under Brazil, Paraguay, and Argentina.

radio, and newspaper headquarters. It is the seat of government, and more than two-thirds of Uruguay's industry is located in or near the capital.

Montevideo was founded in 1726 on a promontory near a large bay that forms a perfect natural harbor. It has gentle hills sloping to the sea. The main street runs along the back of a ridge of hills, the Cuchilla Grande. Across the bay from the Old City is the Cerro de Montevideo (Lookout Mountain) or Montevideo Hill, which gave the city its name. Montevideo, considered one of the loveliest of cosmopolitan cities, is characterized by broad boulevards, parks, and stately buildings.

OTHER CITIES AND TOWNS The next largest cities in Uruguay are Salto (population about 99,072) and Paysandú (population about 73,272), both located along the Río Uruguay. Those cities have developed as a result of

The first thing in Uruguay named by Europeans was the wide estuary where some of South America's major rivers empty into the Atlantic Ocean. This was inappropriately called the Río de la Plata (River of Silver) by the first explorers in 1500. There was no silver in the area, so historians speculate that the Spaniards named the river in hopes that it would lead to riches in the interior. When Spain established a colony at the site of present-day Buenos Aires, they named the area of Argentina, Bolivia, Uruguay, and Paraguay the Viceroyalty of the Río de la Plata. During the colonial period, present-day Uruguay was known as the Banda Oriental, or the East Bank, because of its location east of the estuary. Uruguay struggled against Brazil from 1816 to 1820 before it was, in 1821, annexed to Brazil, whereupon it was called Cisplatine Province. Finally, in 1828, Uruguay gained its independence from Buenos Aires, Brazil, and Spain, and took the name República Oriental del Uruguay. The name Uruguay comes from the indigenous Guaraní language and means "river of the painted birds."

Montevideo was named by one of Ferdinand Magellan's crew in 1520. As they were sailing up the estuary, the lookout saw the conical hill of Montevideo and cried out "Monte vide eu" (I see a mountain).

During the 19th century, two factions fought for control of the new country. For 13 years (1838—51), one group laid siege to Montevideo, while the other defended it. During the war and afterward, the city was known as the Modern Troy because, like Troy of ancient Greece, it was forced to defend itself in a civil war.

farming and trade with Argentina. Salto has benefited from the construction of a hydroelectric dam just north of the city, while Paysandú was given a huge boost by the construction of the General Artigas Bridge that connects Uruguay with Argentina.

The waterfront towns of Colonia del Sacramento and Punta del Este are both prime tourist destinations. Colonia del Sacramento, in the province of Colonia, was originally founded by Portuguese settlers in 1680 and is the oldest city in Uruguay. Punta del Este was founded in 1829 and was known as Villa Ituzaingó before its name was changed. The popular resort town attracts many local and foreign tourists during the summer and is growing steadily.

HISTORY

Tourists look over the wall of a fortress built in the 18th century at Santa Teresa National Park.

THE HISTORY OF URUGUAY has been affected by its geographic position between Argentina and Brazil. Nevertheless, Uruguay has maintained a distinct identity and for most of the 20th century achieved unparalleled levels of education and well-being for its citizens.

URUGUAY BEFORE THE SPANISH

Uruguay is the only country in South America today that has no surviving indigenous people. The first archaeological evidence of human settlement in the area that was to become Uruguay is 8,000 years old. Those earliest inhabitants hunted animals and gathered plant and animal resources in order to survive. From around 4,000 to 8,000 years ago, the stone tools these hunter-gatherers used became more sophisticated, and they also developed the use of the bow and arrow. By 2,000 years ago archaeological evidence suggests the existence of three distinct groups—the Chaná, the Guaraní, and the Charrúa. Those early peoples were all still present at the time of the European discovery of the territory in the 1500s.

THE CHANÁ were hunter-gatherers who supplemented their diet with fishing. They used the bow and arrow, and they smoked fish to preserve it. They moved about in small groups and were highly nomadic. Not much is known of the Chaná because they disappeared soon after the Spaniards started to settle in Uruguay.

The European discovery and settlement of Uruguay forever determined the country's history. Today Uruguay has no surviving indigenous groups and its population is mostly of European descent. Europeans remained in Uruguay for about 300 years before José Gervasio Artigas began to agitate for independence, which was finally won in 1828.

THE GUARANÍ also made a quick exit from the area, but much more is known about their way of life because they are a large cultural group that still exists in other parts of South America. The Guaraní were "shifting" cultivators. They planted crops in small garden plots in the forest, and they would periodically shift, or change fields, to avoid depleting the soil. They also hunted and gathered to supplement their diet. They arrived in the area of the Río de la Plata about 200 years before the Europeans, and few survived the first colonial settlement.

THE CHARRÚA were also hunter-gatherers who used the bow and arrow. Unlike the Chaná, however, some of these clever people survived into the 19th century and played an important role in the wars of independence against Spain. One of their most enduring legacies is the bola or *boleadora* (boh-lay-ah-DOR-ah), a weapon made of rocks that are attached to long leather thongs. The hunter swings the bola above his head (much like a cowboy twirling his lariat) and then releases it spinning through the air to wrap around the neck or legs of the hunted animal. The rocks would either kill the animal outright or at least hobble it. This device was adopted later by the Spaniards for rounding up horses and cattle on the open plains. The Charrúa were able hunters and fighters and managed in part to survive by hunting as game the cattle introduced by the Spaniards in the 1600s. The last band of Charrúas was decimated at the Massacre of Salsipuedes in 1831.

DISAPPEARANCE OF THE INDIGENOUS POPULATION It is estimated that there were about 9,000 Charrúa and 6,000 Chaná and Guaraní Indians at the time of contact with Europeans in the 1500s. By the time of independence, some 300 years later, there were only about 500 Indians remaining in Uruguay. There were three main causes for the disintegration and disappearance of their cultures: disease, intentional extermination, and assimilation.

In the late 1500s and early 1600s, Europeans actually believed that the indigenous peoples of the New World were not fully human. Thus they set out to kill or enslave them. The original people in Uruguay were generally

The Guaraní grew corn, beans, cotton, and yerba maté (YAYR-bah mah-TAY). Maté, a tea made from the leaves and shoots of this shrub, is a stimulant containing caffeine. The beverage was later assimilated into the European culture of Uruguay.

good fighters and were much more effective with their lances and arrows than the Spaniards were with their short-range, clumsy, and inaccurate guns. Disease was the cause of much of the decline in Indian populations. Europeans unleashed many devastating diseases upon the New World, including influenza, syphilis, tuberculosis, and smallpox. With no immunity to these diseases, the original people were soon decimated.

Finally, some Indians were herded into settlements run by religious groups. The goal of the priests was to convert them to Roman Catholicism and change their way of life. As most of Uruguay's original people were nomadic, they hated the confinement and rarely stayed long in those cramped places—in a sense, making them more vulnerable to being hunted down by other Spaniards.

EUROPEAN DISCOVERY AND SETTLEMENT (1502–1810)

As early as 1502 Europeans had sighted Río de la Plata but did not explore the river farther. Then in 1516 Juan Díaz de Solís led a Spanish expedition up the estuary. They thought they had found the tip of South America when they landed about 70 miles (113 km) east of modern Montevideo. The landing party was killed instantly by Charrúas, and the remaining crew abandoned the site. The Spaniards attempted to found settlements along various rivers throughout the 1500s but were repeatedly repelled by Indian attacks.

In 1580 they established a foothold with the second founding of Buenos Aires. In 1603 Governor Hernando Arias of Asunción, in present-day Paraguay, ordered that cattle and horses be released into the grasslands of Uruguay. The animals multiplied and attracted Buenos Aires ranchers, who crossed the river to capture the herds; but they never settled permanently on the Uruguayan side.

The Portuguese were the first people to be successful in settling Uruguay. They founded the city of Colonia del Sacramento along the Río de la Plata opposite Buenos Aires in 1680. In response to that, the Spaniards founded Montevideo farther east along the estuary in 1726.

The decline of the original peoples through diseases introduced by Europeans continues to this day, as the few remaining indigenous groups of the Amazon jungle come into contact with nonindigenous peoples.

Argentine historian Diego Lascano holding metal fragments of French muskets and a broken British six-pounder cannonball.

INDEPENDENCE (1810–28)

The hero of the story of Uruguayan independence is General José Gervasio Artigas (1764–1850). He was the first to organize an army with the purpose of freeing Uruguay from Spain, Buenos Aires, and Brazilian interests. In 1810 fighting started in Buenos Aires between two factions: those who wanted Buenos Aires and all of Río de la Plata to sever ties to Spain and those who wanted to remain loyal to the Spanish crown.

General Artigas led the fight against the Spaniards with a ragtag band of Indians and ranchers, joining the revolt against the Spanish in 1810 and 1811. They successfully expelled the Spanish governor from Montevideo in 1814.

JOSÉ ARTIGAS: URUGUAY'S GEORGE WASHINGTON

José Gervasio Artigas was born in Montevideo in 1764. His family was prominent and wealthy, and he was educated by Franciscan friars. His experiences working with the gauchos, or ordinary cowboys, taught him to love the countryside and the common people. He joined the fighting when the first independence movement flared up in Buenos Aires in 1810. He had his first military success against the forces loyal to Spain in 1811 at the Battle of Las Piedras. When a peace agreement was reached between independence fighters and Spanish loyalists in 1811, Artigas refused to abide by it because it implied that Uruguay would return to Spanish rule. He took his army on a long march away from Montevideo, called the Exodus of the Orientals (those from the east bank of the river). They were joined by 16,000 other patriots who supported his cause. In 1813 he wrote a document known as "Instructions of Year 13", which outlined the principles of independence and confederation for Uruguay. He eventually was forced to leave Uruguay when the Brazilians took over in 1820. Exiled to Paraguay, where he remained until his death in 1850, José Artigas is recognized as the father of Uruguayan independence.

Brazil decided to invade Uruguay, sensing that the newly liberated territory had been weakened by the revolution. In 1816 Artigas managed to repel a Brazilian attack, but by 1820 the Uruguayan general was defeated. He was exiled and the captured territory was named Cisplatine Province.

The fighting stopped for five years, during which time the British traded freely with the Brazilians for hides. In 1825 a group of 33 exiles from Montevideo, led by Juan Antonio Lavalleja and aided by Argentina, invaded Cisplatine, and fighting for independence flared up again. With such renewed hostilities, the British could not trade in the area and so decided to intervene diplomatically. The Brazilians and the Argentineans, with the help of British diplomacy, finally agreed to the establishment of an independent country between them. The new buffer state became known as the República Oriental del Uruguay and was granted its freedom in 1828. Lavalleja's group became known as the "Oriental 33" for the patriotic exiles' part in aiding the cause of Uruguayan freedom.

THE 19TH CENTURY (1830–1903)

This period was one of great internal political turmoil in Uruguay. The first constitution was established in 1830. General José Fructuoso Rivera, formerly a lieutenant in Artigas's army, became president of the new nation. In 1835 General Manuel Oribe succeeded Rivera as president. But in 1838 Rivera deposed Oribe and took over Montevideo. Oribe sought help from Buenos Aires and came back to lay siege to Montevideo. From 1839 to 1851 the two forces fought over Montevideo in what became known as the Guerra Grande, or Long War.

At one battle, the two sides each distinguished themselves with different colored hatbands: Oribe's forces wore white (*blanco*), while Rivera's wore red (*colorado*). Rivera's supporters tended to be urban-based and later formed a political party known as the Colorados, while Oribe's supporters were rural-based and formed the Partido Blanco.

From the end of the Long War until 1903—more than 50 years—the two hostile factions continued to fight and to struggle for the control of Uruguay's politics. At the end of the 19th century, after a series of conflicts and treaties, a system of sharing power between the two dominant parties was devised. That system, known as coparticipation, affected Uruguayan politics throughout the 20th century.

Montevideo founder Don Bruno Mauricio de Zabala commands the view in Plaza Zabala.

THE TRIPLE ALLIANCE   Apart from the internal struggles, Uruguay also engaged in a war against Paraguay called the War of the Triple Alliance. Francisco Solano López, then the dictator of Paraguay, threatened Uruguayan independence, claiming he would take a port on the Río de la Plata for his country. In 1864 the Triple Alliance of Brazil, Argentina, and Uruguay went to war against Paraguay. The Paraguayans were outnumbered 10 to 1, and after six years of fighting, the Paraguayan population was virtually decimated. The war ended in 1870 with Paraguay totally defeated.

MODERN URUGUAY

BATLLE AND BATLLISMO (1903—66) José Batlle (bahj-jay) y Ordóñez served as president during two periods, 1903—07 and 1911—15. During those eight years he initiated far-reaching reforms that determined the future of Uruguay for more than 60 years. His legacy of political, social, and economic reform is known as Batllismo (bahj-JEES-moh).

President Batlle believed the Uruguayan economy was too small to be left in the hands of private interests, especially when such interests were foreign. So he began "autonomous entities," which were government-owned industries with monopolies over certain types of manufacturing or export goods. Since they were under the control of the government, these industries could be taxed according to need and the rights of workers would be protected.

Distinctive European architecture illustrates Europe's influence on Uruguay.

He also believed that politics and religion should be separated; as a result, divorce became a purely civil matter. Among his more important reforms are the following: abolition of income tax for low-paid public employees (1905); establishment of secondary schools in every major city (1906); the right of women to sue for divorce on grounds of cruelty (1907); establishment of state banks (1912); creation of an autonomous agency to run the port of Montevideo (1912); nationalization of the telephone utility (1915); provision of credit to the rural poor through state banks; and drafting a new constitution. The constitution was adopted after his second term in 1919.

Perhaps Batlle's most enduring legacy was a system of government he created called the *colegiado* (koh-lay-hee-AH-doh), or collegium system. Between 1907 and 1911 he traveled extensively in Europe, and was most impressed with the Swiss system of government in which there is no single

The headquarters of the Communist Party in Uruguay in 1941.

THE MASSACRE AT SALSIPUEDES

Ironically, Salsipuedes (SAHL-see-poo-AY-days) means "Get out if you can" and is the name of the place where the last large group of Charrúa Indians were captured or killed outright by European Uruguayans.

After independence from Brazil in 1828, the new government decided that the Indians who had fought so bravely with General José Gervasio Artigas had to be destroyed. The excuse they used was that the Charrúa were stealing settlers' cattle. The president at the time, General Fructuoso Rivera, was trusted by the Charrúa. In 1831 he sent them a message that they were needed by the army to defend the border against the Brazilians at Salsipuedes. When the loyal Indians arrived—some 340 men, women, and children—they set up camp, exchanged gifts with the army officers, and turned in for the night. The army of 1,200 soldiers attacked the group, killing 40 Charrúa fighters outright and capturing the remaining 300. Those Charrúa were forced to march to Montevideo where they were enslaved as household servants. By 1840 there were only 18 surviving Charrúa in Uruguay.

The Charrúa Indians no longer exist as a people. As of the 2001 Argentine census, there were only 676 persons of mixed blood with Charrúa ancestry living in Uruguay.

president but rather a panel of citizens with equal authority in control of the executive. He supported the creation of a new constitution that divided the powers of government between the president and a nine-member collegium with six representatives from the party that won the elections and three from the losing party. In a sense, that was a continuation of the 19th-century struggle for coparticipation between the two big political parties. The new constitution also guaranteed the secret ballot and a system of voting called "double simultaneous balloting." Most of the other politicians of the time rejected the collegial idea, but when Batlle threatened to run for the presidency a third time if they did not pass the constitution, they agreed to accept the concept.

Democracy, loosely defined, was maintained throughout that period, but competition for control of the collegium and efforts to abolish it by both parties continued. During the Great Depression (1930s), there was a brief suspension of elections while two factions, one from each party, tried to control the government. With large increases in exports resulting

José Batlle was born into a strong Colorado Party family. His father, Lorenzo Batlle y Grau, served as president from 1868 to 1872. Batlle himself founded a Colorado newspaper, *El Día*, in 1886 and wrote about politics throughout his life.

from the Korean War (1950–53), however, democracy was revived. Uruguay had one of the most stable regimes in Latin America throughout the first half of the 20th century. All that serenity was to change in the 1960s.

REPRESSION AND DICTATORSHIP

(1966–84) Although Batllismo had created a relatively stable government with an educated population protected by a large social welfare system, it also left a legacy of extravagant government spending. When the export economy was booming, that deep pocket worked fine, but when there were slowdowns in the demand for Uruguay's main exports (beef, hides, and wool), the government was left with huge expenditures and little income. That meant heavy borrowing, resulting in inflation. The cost of living for Uruguayans doubled between 1959 and 1962, doubling again between 1962 and 1964. Inflation skyrocketed to 100 percent by 1965. People wanted change, starting with the collegial system.

The Colorados won the election of 1967 under General Oscar Gestido, who soon abolished the collegium and awarded more powers to himself as the president. When Gestido died later that same year, his vice president, Areco Pacheco, took power and began to outlaw various left-wing groups, newspapers, and small political parties that had sprung up in response to the economic crisis.

Former Tupamaro guerrilla and one of the leaders of the Frente Amplio party, Jose Mujica is shown speaking at an election rally.

THE TUPAMAROS

The populist group Tupamaros was founded in 1963 under the leadership of socialist law student Raul Sendic. He became involved with the plight of poor agricultural workers and vowed to help them against a government that refused to increase their wages despite high inflation. Aside from some small marches and thefts of food, the Tupamaros did not rise as a real threat until the mid-1960s when they began robbing banks to fund their activities. They practiced a policy of not harming innocent people during their raids, thus gaining wide popular support. They wanted the government to stop repressing workers and quit taking loans and orders from foreign powers, specifically the United States. Many Uruguayans felt that change was needed, and force seemed the only way to make it happen.

Tupamaro (too-pah-MAH-roh) is a short version of Tupac Amaru, the name of an Incan chief who led a rebellion against the Spanish colonial government in Peru in 1780. He was captured and drawn and quartered (disemboweled and pulled apart by the limbs), and has been a symbol of political activism for South American dissidents since that time.

Repression and suspension of civil rights continued and intensified in the late 1960s in reaction to a newly formed revolutionary group called the Tupamaros. That group began an armed struggle against the government, believing it was selling out Uruguay to foreign interests at the cost of Uruguayans' well-being. They were responsible for many acts of terrorism, but the two most notable were the kidnappings of Daniel Mitrione, an American, in 1970, and Geoffrey Jackson, the British ambassador, in 1971.

While most Uruguayans did not want violence, there was a growing sense that a new political party was needed to represent the people. In the 1971 election, a new group called the Frente Amplio (Broad Front) ran for power. This was a coalition of left-wing political groups headed by Liber Seregi. To the shock and dismay of the other two more conservative parties, the Frente Amplio took 30 percent of the vote in Montevideo and 18 percent of the national vote. Juan María Bordaberry of the Colorados was sworn in as president in 1972, but many voters suspected fraud.

Over 60,000 people were arrested or detained during the period of repression. In 1979 Amnesty International estimated that 20 percent of Uruguayans had been imprisoned at one time or another.

During the whole period of government repression, the military had been quietly growing in strength and power and was increasing its pressure on the president to do things its way. For the first two years of Bordaberry's presidency, the military stayed in the wings trying to control him indirectly, but in 1973 it lost its patience and, in a coup, deposed Bordaberry and established a dictatorship. The main causes for the military takeover were economic decline, social unrest among workers and students, terrorism wielded by the Tupamaros, and weak and ineffective politicians. By 1973 the military had effectively wiped out the Tupamaros, but it continued to target them as an excuse to justify their rampant abuse of civil rights.

During the dictatorship, the number of military and police personnel nearly doubled to an all-time high of 64,000 in 1978, and they were used to keep Uruguayans in a state of constant fear through grave human rights abuses. As a result, 10 percent of Uruguayans left the country, never to return. The education system was virtually dismantled; 80 percent of university professors and 40—50 percent of public school teachers were

There was a pervasive military presence in Uruguay after 1973.

arrested, fired, or fled their jobs in fear of torture.

One of the goals of the military government was to improve Uruguay's economy. Unfortunately, it came into power just as the worldwide oil crisis started in 1973, when the oil-producing nations decided to raise the price of gas and oil. Every country dependent on imported oil suffered during that time, and those with their own oil industry tried to generate more money by protecting it through trade tariffs. The Uruguayan military thought it could stimulate the economy by opening it to foreign investment. That only made things worse, as small Uruguayan companies could not compete and went under. Government spending on social programs was cut and wages were frozen, which increased poverty. Continued loss of income from falling exports resulted in heavy borrowing from international banks; by 1981 Uruguay's debt was $4 billion. With a population of only 3 million, that sum was staggering!

RETURN TO DEMOCRACY (1984–PRESENT)

The end of military rule began in 1980 with the failure of a plebiscite organized by the military that would have guaranteed their continued power. Elections were promised for 1984, though the military still insisted

A mounted gaucho riding to Pueblo Celestino to cast his vote. The road back to democracy in Uruguay has been long.

that certain left-wing parties could not participate. Faced with worsening economic conditions, however, the military reluctantly gave back power and responsibility to civilian leaders. Eventually the three main parties and the military agreed on a new constitution, and elections were held in 1984 as planned.

The presidential election of 1984 was won by the Colorado Battlista candidate, Julio María Sanguinetti, who had gained power only on the sufferance of the generals. Against popular demands for criminal trials and retribution, Sanguinetti granted the military a blanket amnesty for their human rights abuses of the previous eleven years.

The challenges for subsequent democratic governments have been to revive an economy suffering from an incredible debt burden and vocal labor unrest; to rebuild the education system after years of neglect; to mediate between the military and groups who want to see them tried and jailed for their crimes; and to continue to support a large military budget to prevent another coup. Since 1984, politics have not been calm in Uruguay, though democracy has survived. The military has continued to be a threat to civilian rule through indirect pressures applied to the president.

In 1989 the Blanco Party returned to power. Five years later, however, in 1994, Julio María Sanguinetti, of the Colorado Battlista, won a second term. The margin was extremely narrow, with Sanguinetti taking 31.40 percent of the votes, followed by Alberto Volonte with 30.20 percent, Tabaré Vázquez with 30.02 percent, and Rafael Michelini with 5.04 percent. The result was a coalition government that reflected the wish of the Uruguayans to return to their traditional democracy.

The most significant event in 1991 was the launch of MERCOSUR (Mercado Común del Cono Sur, or Southern Cone Common Market). The state parties involved were Uruguay, Brazil, Argentina, and Paraguay.

Ministers of Economy representing MERCOSUR from different nations gather for a conference.

Elected Uruguay's president in 2004, Tabaré Vázquez, a popular leftist, is also a medical doctor.

The purpose of MERCOSUR was to help the respective populations' trading among themselves by promoting scientific and technological developments and improving the quality of goods and services. Nevertheless, bilateral ties with Argentina later became strained over the construction in 2005 of a large wood pulp mill in Uruguay on a shared river.

Uruguay's first leftist president, Dr. Tabaré Vázquez, a cancer specialist, took office in 2005. The coalition he led, the Broad Front (Frente Amplio), also called the Progressive Encounter (Encuentro Progresista), was composed of former guerrillas, socialists, communists, and independent leftists. He won on the promise to improve a stagnant economy, bring greater social justice to Uruguay, and deal with the legacy of human rights violations during the 1973—85 military dictatorship. The Vázquez administration made good on this promise and uncovered important forensic evidence of prior abuses during his first three years in office. One of his first acts as president was to announce a $100-million-a-year National Emergency Plan to assist the estimated 20 percent of Uruguayans mired in abject poverty.

GOVERNMENT

The Palacio Legislativo (National Congress) building in Montevideo.

F OR MOST OF THE 20TH CENTURY, Uruguay had maintained a consistently democratic governmental system with two traditional parties. After the military dictatorship collapse in the 1980s and the subsequent return to democracy, the nation has shouldered many difficulties and new parties have emerged to challenge traditional leadership.

STRUCTURE OF GOVERNMENT

EXECUTIVE Uruguay is a constitutional republic. The president is the chief of state and head of government, and he is aided by a vice president and a council of ministers appointed by the president with approval of the General Assembly. Both the president and vice president are elected by popular vote for five-year terms and may not serve consecutive terms.

The council of ministers includes the following 10 ministries: interior; foreign affairs; economy and finance; transportation and public works; health; labor and social security; livestock, agriculture, and fisheries; education and culture; defense; industry, energy, and mining; tourism; and territorial regulation and environment.

LEGISLATIVE There is a bicameral General Assembly that provides checks and balances of the president's authority: the Chamber of

After a painful period under a repressive dictatorship and military rule, Uruguay finally reverted to democracy. The people elect the president, who then appoints the vice president and cabinet of ministers. A unique aspect of the electoral process is the double simultaneous ballot system. In 2004 Tabaré Vásquez was elected president of Uruguay.

THE URUGUAYAN FLAG

The flag of Uruguay was designed and approved in 1830. There are four light blue stripes alternating with five white ones. Those are the colors of Argentina and symbolize Uruguay's connection with Buenos Aires during colonial times. There is also a white patch with the Sun of May emblazoned in gold upon it. The Sun of May has 16 rays that are alternately straight and wavy, symbolizing independence from their Spanish overlords in May 1810.

Senators (Camara de Senadores) consists of 30 elected representatives headed by the vice president, and the Chamber of Deputies (Camara de Diputados) consists of 99 elected representatives. There are 19 departments (administrative subdivisions), each with an elected governor. Uruguay's departments are not like states, since their autonomy is quite limited. Most decisions are made by the national government.

The military has remained relatively strong since its dictatorship succumbed, but it is now subject to presidential control through the minister of defense. Military service is voluntary, in any of the three branches of the service: army, navy, and air force.

The national flag of Uruguay.

A person may be elected president only if he or she has not served in that position for at least three months prior to the election. This serves to prevent an incumbent and his party from taking over the position for life. Elections are held every five years, and all government positions are elected simultaneously and proportionally. Everyone over 18 years of age is eligible to vote. Voting in Uruguay is very confusing since it combines primary and final elections. This is called the double simultaneous ballot, which is explained below.

The Uruguayan constitution provides for direct public participation in governmental decisions. If ordinary citizens are unhappy with a decision, they can force the government to hold a national referendum to resolve it. That means that the troubling issue is put to all voters to decide. To do that, 25 percent of eligible voters must first sign a petition requesting the referendum. Once that number of signatures is gathered, the government must then hold the vote within 60 days and abide by the results.

Double Simultaneous Ballot

When an election is held, every political party may run more than one candidate for the office of president. People vote for their choice as usual, but the tricky part pops up when the votes are counted. The winner is not the person with a simple majority of votes but the person with the most votes from the party with the most votes!

Let us take an example to demonstrate how this works. To make it simple, assume that only two parties, the Colorados and Blancos, are running candidates for office, and that each of them offers two candidates for president. When the votes are counted, the totals are as follows:

Colorados		Blancos	
Candidate A	25	Candidate C	10
Candidate B	30	Candidate D	35
Total	55		45

(continued)

Candidate D has the simple majority of votes, but the Colorados got the most votes of the two parties, therefore one of their candidates will win—the one with the greater number of votes, Candidate B. Obviously, election returns are scrutinized with care.

JUDICIARY There are five members in the Supreme Court of Justice, who are chosen by the executive and serve for 10-year terms. They may be reappointed after a break of five years. The Supreme Court appoints all other judges in the country. The Appellate Tribunals, each composed of three judges, form the next-highest judicial level, followed by lower courts.

In addition, there are electoral and administrative (contentious) courts, an accounts court, and a military judicial system.

POLITICAL PARTIES

Uruguay has a multiparty political system with three main players in modern elections: the Blancos; the Colorado Party, which has held the presidency almost continuously since independence; and the Frente Amplio, which has emerged as a coalition of fairly radical left-wing groups.

The land-owning Blanco Party, which is also known as the National Party, was formed under General Manuel Oribe in the 19th century. It tends to represent the rural and conservative elements of the population. It was the Blancos (whites) that forced President Batlle to include proportional representation and the secret ballot in the constitution of 1919. Although they are considered the second largest party and the traditional opponents of the Colorados, they have held the presidency only three times since Uruguay's independence from Brazil: 1835—38, 1958—67, and 1989—94.

The Colorado Party tends to represent the urban middle class, which is the largest group in Uruguay. Batlle shaped the party into a mature political organ, but his radical reforms also split the party into factions. Some of his party members supported his ideas of a collegial system, while others did not. Although the collegial system has long been abandoned in Uruguay, those

The double simultaneous ballot affects how political parties are run. The different factions within each political party may represent widely different ideas and platforms. In other words, citizens who are very conservative may vote for a candidate from one of the parties, while liberal people may vote for a different candidate from the same party.

egalitarian factions in the Colorado Party still exist. The Frente Amplio or Broad Front, a party made up of a coalition of many smaller parties and party factions, was formed in 1971 to oppose increasing repression by the government. In the 1971 election, the Frente Amplio won 18.3 percent of the vote, but once the military took power, the party was outlawed. The Frente leaders were jailed or went into exile during the dictatorship. When democracy returned in 1984, Frente Amplio won 21.3 percent of the popular vote, demonstrating that its support was growing. The party is quite left-wing, including communists, socialists, Christian Democrats, and radical splinter groups from the two major parties.

The Communist Party became an official party in 1921 and has always been considered very radical. Its members were founding members of the Frente Amplio in 1971. During the dictatorship and its first election, the Communist Party was outlawed. The government did recognize it in 1985, and in the 1989 election the communists won about 10 percent of the vote.

A resident of Montevideo shows his support for President Vásquez.

The socialists were organized as a party in 1910, but in 1921 a majority of the members broke away to form the more radical Communist Party. Throughout the 20th century the socialists became increasingly left-wing, opposing foreign investment in Uruguay, for example. Some members of the Socialist Party helped form the Tupamaros, the armed guerrilla group. The socialists are still part of the Frente Amplio coalition.

Finally, there is the Christian Democratic Party, the first Roman Catholic political party in Uruguay. It was founded in 1910. Traditionally, it has not received more than 3–5 percent of the vote. It joined with the Frente Amplio coalition in 1971 and again in 1984. It left the coalition in 1989, however, but rejoined when a new coalition, Encuentro Progresista-Frente Amplio, was formed in 1994. The Christian Democratic Party is now part of the Alianza Progresista coalition that formed in 1999.

CURRENT POLITICAL SITUATION

The major challenge to Uruguay since the economic crisis of 2002 is the reorganization of the political, social, and economic aspects of the country. In the presidential election held in November 2004, the Frente Amplio won the contest, indicating that the urban middle class is increasingly supportive of left-wing politics. The new administration under the leadership of President Tabaré Vázquez has developed an innovative national strategy on six complementary pillars: enhancing productivity, fostering social development, encouraging innovation, strengthening democracy, improving regional and global integration, and promoting policies that consolidate and promote Uruguayan culture.

The first steps taken by the Vásquez government had a positive effect on the country, which was recovering steadily from the 2002 economic crisis. The administration undertook a series of structural reforms, expanded the social assistance network, and provided equal opportunities to its citizens.

Generally, the Colorados are considered to be more liberal than the Blancos, but even so, it was a Colorado president, Juan María Bordaberry, who allowed the military to gain enormous power in Uruguay in the early 1970s.

Supporters of the ruling party, Frente Amplio.

TABARÉ VÁZQUEZ: URUGUAY'S FIRST LEFT-WING PRESIDENT

Tabaré Ramón Vázquez Rosas, from the Broad Front coalition, defeated the ruling Colorado Party presidential candidate to become Uruguay's head of state in March 2005. His victory reflected a regional trend of left-wing governments in Brazil, Venezuela, Chile, and Argentina.

President Vázquez, a cancer specialist doctor and also a former mayor of Montevideo, promised to alleviate poverty. On taking office, he announced a $100 million emergency plan to help the poor. In 2005 the government faced protests from Uruguayans who thought that the poverty plan was not being carried out quickly enough. Despite this, Vázquez remains popular with the people. His current term will end in 2010.

ECONOMY

A worker harvesting grapes in a vineyard in Juanico, in the department of Canelones.

CHAPTER 4

URUGUAY HAS A SPECIAL geographic and historical position as the buffer between Argentina and Brazil. Those two countries are giants in physical size, population, and economic production compared with Uruguay. Uruguay has very few natural resources. It does not have large forests or mines, and much of its land is unsuited to growing crops.

For that reason, the original settlers turned to livestock production, which is a very significant part of the economy even today. Uruguay's

Livestock production continues to be an important factor in Uruguay's economy.

The political strife in the early years of Uruguay's independence caused its economy great instability. Nonetheless, the government has been working to get the economy back on track. Uruguay's main exports are in livestock and agricultural products and their related goods. Uruguay is also part of a South American free trade agreement called MERCOSUR.

population is too small to support a big industrial sector. All these factors have made it difficult for Uruguay to sustain economic growth.

In addition, Uruguay generally imports more goods such as cars and machinery from Brazil and Argentina than it exports food to them. That results in trade deficits because the country is losing money by having to spend more on imports than it earns from exports. From 1999 to 2002 the economy suffered a major setback when Argentina made large withdrawals of U.S. dollars deposited in Uruguayan banks. This led to a nosedive of the Uruguayan peso and a massive rise in unemployment to 19.4 percent.

Since Batlle's reforms at the beginning of the 20th century (except for the period of military dictatorship), the government has tried to provide its people with a good education at a reasonable cost and other welfare benefits, such as wage protection and social security for retired people.

Uruguay was able to recover from the 2002 economic crisis that had left over 30 percent of its population in poverty and a huge external debt. The International Monetary Fund (IMF) guided Uruguay to stem further damage. By 2004 the economy started to improve. High commodity prices for Uruguay's exports, a strong peso, growth in the region, and low international interest rates improved its debt profile. It managed to pay off $1.1 billion in IMF debt.

By 2008 unemployment had receded to only 7.6 percent. An outstanding issue—the migration of Uruguayan youth—continues to challenge the administration. Educated and eager to work, many young citizens seek better opportunities in other countries.

CURRENCY

The currency in Uruguay is called the peso Uruguayo, or Uruguayan peso. It is divided into 100 *centésimos*, or cents. Because of inflation and soaring prices, in 1993 the currency was changed, so that 1,000 of the old pesos became one new peso. With the new currency, prices were affordable again and the currency was stronger on the international market. One U.S. dollar was worth 24.5 Uruguayan pesos at 2009 rates of exchange.

A rice field being harvested with a combine harvester. The export of rice is a major component of Uruguay's economy.

MAIN INDUSTRIES

AGRICULTURE Agricultural products are the primary source of exports. About 41 million acres (16.6 million hectares) of land are devoted to agriculture, and approximately 90 percent of that land is used to raise animals that provide meat and dairy products, wool, hides, and leather goods. Uruguay has over 11.2 million sheep (2006), and 12.1 million head of cattle (2007). The nation produces rice, wheat, soybeans, and barley as well as peaches, oranges, tangerines, and pears.

There are three agricultural zones in the country: the southern zone, which produces fruit and vegetables for consumers living in Montevideo and for export; the northern zone, where the sheep and cattle ranches are situated; and the eastern zone, where grains and cereals are grown.

About 52 percent of all exports come directly from agricultural production (rice and raw meat, for example) or indirectly from manufacturing of agricultural goods, for instance, canned meat and leather products. Agricultural products bring in about $5 billion (2007 estimate) of the total earnings in any given year. Other economic activity includes mining of semiprecious stones such as amethyst and topaz, fishing, hydroelectric power production, and forestry.

MANUFACTURING Although agriculture accounts for most exports, manufacturing and construction contribute 32 percent of the country's total income in a given year. The main manufacturing industries are meatpacking, oil refining, manufacturing of cement, food and beverage processing, leather and cloth manufacturing, and chemical processing. Still, manufacturing depends on farming, since many of the factories process food or produce clothing made from wool and leather.

SERVICE SECTOR The lion's share of the national economy is generated by the service sector. That includes businesses such as restaurants, hotels, transportation, community services, communications, and any other service that people pay for in daily life—a haircut or housecleaning. One of the services Uruguay offers to the world is its special banking system. Banks in Uruguay, like those in Switzerland, keep all accounts completely private; no one can find out who has money in them or how much they have. The service sector accounts for about 58 percent of the country's total income every year.

A leatherworker making a pair of boots.

Since the 1980s, one of the biggest and most persistent problems faced by all countries in South America is their foreign debt. Just like individuals who go to banks to borrow money in order to buy a house or a car, countries go to special international banks, such as the World Bank, to borrow money. When you borrow from a bank, you have to agree to pay back the money with interest over a certain length of time. Uruguay, like many of its neighbors, faces a debt crisis because it owes far more money than it can earn. To give some idea of how serious this is, in 1985 Uruguay, with a population then of almost 3 million, owed $4.9 billion dollars. If the debt were shared, each Uruguayan man, woman, and child would owe about $1,600 to foreign banks. Since the minimum wage is only about $90 per month—and many do not work at all—this is a crushing debt burden.

When a country cannot afford to pay back its loans, the IMF steps in. It tells the country what to do in order to make enough money to pay back its debt. That usually involves cutbacks in spending, limits on wages and prices, and curtailed social services. The government of Uruguay tried to do that itself in 1990, but the people protested. The whole debt situation is responsible for many of the labor problems in Uruguay and in all of Latin America today. Nevertheless, in 2006 Uruguay managed to pay off a billion-dollar debt to the IMF.

INTERNATIONAL TRADE

Uruguay's primary trade partners are Brazil, Argentina, the United States, Mexico, and Germany. The biggest export commodities are live animals and animal products such as milk, meat, fish, furs, wool, woolen cloth and clothing, and hides and leather products; also rice, vegetables, processed food and drinks. The main imports from the partner countries include machinery, vehicles, fuels such as oil and gas, and chemicals. Uruguay's position as primarily an agricultural country with few natural resources of its own is reflected in its trade.

In 1991 a new trade agreement between Uruguay, Paraguay, Brazil, and Argentina came into effect. MERCOSUR, commonly called Mercado Común del Cono Sur, or Southern Market, is a free-trade agreement wherein participating countries trade with one another without charging any taxes on imports and exports. For a small country like Uruguay, MERCOSUR means that no added taxes are levied on food and clothing exports to the large populations of Brazil and Argentina. If Uruguay can produce a pound of meat more cheaply than Brazil, then its meat will sell more cheaply in Brazilian supermarkets. This is a great advantage for all the countries involved. Venezuela is also a full member of the trade bloc now. Chile, Bolivia, Colombia, Ecuador, and Peru are associate members of MERCOSUR, without full voting rights or complete access to the markets of MERCOSUR's full members. This makes the total population of producers and consumers bigger still.

ENERGY, TRANSPORTATION, COMMUNICATIONS

Uruguay generates its own hydroelectric power from dams on its many rivers. One of the largest dams is at Salto Grande on the Río Uruguay. Uruguay needs to import petroleum products from Argentina to supplement its energy supply. The imported crude oil is then refined into usable forms in Uruguay.

Livestock and animal products make up a large portion of Uruguay's exports. Sheep, like these being auctioned, are part of that vital industry.

Uruguay has one of the best highway systems in all of South America. Of the 48,000 miles (77,249 km) of roads, some 90 percent are rural dirt roads; the rest are paved or graveled. The railway system is owned by the government and is used primarily for transporting goods rather than people. The principal shipping ports are Montevideo, Punta del Este, Colonia, Fray Bentos, Paysandú, and Salto. There are two international airports: Montevideo and Punta del Este. For travel within the country, there are seven smaller airports with permanent runways, and 51 others with unpaved runways.

Most telecommunications facilities are centered in Montevideo, where the majority of the people live. With over 965,200 (2007) telephones in operation, Uruguay has one of the highest number of telephones per capita in South America.

LABOR FORCE

There are just over 1.631 million workers in Uruguay (2007 estimate), of whom 40 percent are women. Uruguayans are considered to be the best-educated workforce in Latin America. The national retirement age is 60, and the average wage is about $966 per month. The following is the 2007 distribution of workers in the various sectors: 76 percent in the service sector, 15 percent in industry, and 9 percent in agriculture. Unemployment was 9.2 percent.

Workers have been organized into unions since the 19th century. The unions have been quite effective in obtaining good working conditions and wages for their members. In the mid-20th century, many unions were associated with the Communist Party, but by the 1960s fewer than 3 percent of union members were affiliated with the party. Increasing repression in the late 1960s included the suppression of labor activities and the harassment of labor leaders. The military simply banned unions and strikes during the dictatorship. The return of democracy in 1984 opened the doors to a return of the unions.

Rural workers make up a scant 9 percent of the total labor force and often are forced to live in shantytowns and toil for low wages on big farms.

With inflation, prices shoot up quickly while wages do not. Hence a person's "real" wage falls because it does not buy as much food or clothing as it did before.

ENVIRONMENT

The Ombu tree is indigenous to Uruguay.

URUGUAY IS ADMIRED FOR BEING one of the least polluted countries in South America. Expanding city populations and industries, however, have resulted in environmental problems such as compromised clean water sources, inefficient waste disposal, and destruction of natural habitats.

WATER AND SANITATION

The meatpacking and tannery industries may make Uruguay's economy more competitive. At the same time, the country is finding ways to reduce

Sheep pelts drying on racks.

Uruguay is one of the least polluted countries in South America. Its livestock and agricultural production industries mean that the country has to find the delicate balance between preserving and protecting its natural habitats and clearing land for economic uses. To protect its flora and fauna from disappearing, the government has put together a system of protected areas.

water pollution caused by those industries. A 2005—06 livestock survey carried out by the Ministry of Livestock, Agriculture, and Fisheries reported 11.7 million head of cattle and 11.2 million sheep. Almost 3 million cattle were sent to slaughterhouses in that period. Beef production reached over a high of over 600,000 tons. In addition, the number of sheep slaughtered reached 1.4 million.

In 2007 the state-run water utility of Uruguay expanded water and sanitation services to the small towns and outskirts of cities and sought to better manage its performance. Currently 98 percent of the population has access to clean water, one of the highest percentages found in South and Central America.

Another source of substantial pollution and agitation is acid rain from Brazilian industry. Up to one-fifth of the country is affected by acid rain generated in Uruguay's northern neighbor, Brazil.

The city of Montevideo is blanketed in smoke caused by bush fires in Argentina. Aside from its own problems, Uruguay's environment is also affected by its larger neighbors.

AIR POLLUTION

Uruguayans enjoy pure air and deep blue skies as their country has the least environmental pollution in the world.

Like most developing countries, however, the cities of Uruguay are fast filling up with people and are promoting their own industries. The nation takes positive action to reduce the resulting air pollution. One of the ways is to encourage the use of electric cars.

REDUCTION OF NATURAL HABITAT

Rice is a major export of Uruguay. When natural habitats are converted into rice cropland, the most noticeable environmental impact is the extinction of animal and plant species. A total of 11 plant species were listed as threatened in 1996; 7 bird species and 5 mammal species are endangered. The glaucous macaw has become extinct. To address that looming problem, Uruguay has put together a system of protected areas and a management plan to harbor those endangered species and others as they may need to be included.

Uruguay has had to balance the need to convert habitats into croplands and the need to protect its delicate environment.

URUGUAYANS

An Uruguayan man sipping maté from a decorated gourd.

T HE DEMOGRAPHICS OF URUGUAY show some interesting and distinctive features. Demography is the study of the features of human populations, including ethnic composition, age and gender breakdown, average birthrate, and so on. Because of its unusual history, Uruguayan demographics are not typical of Latin America.

ETHNIC GROUPS

Uruguay has one of the most homogeneous populations in South America. The majority— 88 percent of the population—are descendants of European settlers. There are two main groups: those whose forebears were from Spain and those whose ancestors originally came from Italy. Both groups now speak Spanish and intermingle everywhere.

The next largest ethnic group is the mestizos, the descendants of unions between Indians and Spaniards and Italians during colonial times. Mestizos are 8 percent of the population and generally live in rural areas.

Right: Mestizos, like this boy, make up 8 percent of Uruguay's total population.

53

Finally, 4 percent of the population is of African descent. Most of that small group are descended from slaves taken from Africa in the 18th and early 19th centuries. They live mostly in Montevideo where the largest concentration of slaves was. Some members of that African-Uruguayan group, however, came to Uruguay from Brazil, and they live along the northern border with Brazil.

Though Uruguay is an open and tolerant society, some racism persists among different ethnic groups.

IMMIGRATION, MIGRATION, EMIGRATION

As in many New World nations, the bulk of the modern Uruguayan population is descended from immigrants from all over the world. First were the Spaniards, who started settling in Uruguay in the 18th century. The next group to arrive were African slaves, who were used mostly as domestic servants. After abolition, the Africans stayed on to form a small but vital subculture in

Official figures suggest that 180,000 Uruguayans departed for good in the period 1963–75. The peak of outward migration was in 1973–75: 30,000 left in 1973, 60,000 in 1974, and nearly 40,000 in 1975. For the duration of the dictatorship, 1975-85, another 150,000 Uruguayans left the country. Between 1996 and 2002, almost 100,000 skilled workers, 3 percent of the entire population, emigrated during a lengthy recession.

Uruguayan folk dancers. Uruguay has one of the most homogenous populations in South America.

Immigrants make up a large portion of the modern Uruguayan population, like this African-Uruguayan couple.

the country. Argentina was in need of immigrants and sent agents to Italy to recruit settlers. But the Italians did not know much about South America and often confused Argentina and Uruguay. In 1890 the Uruguayan government actively encouraged immigration by promising able-bodied arrivals food and shelter for eight days after landing and free transportation to the interior of the country. Consequently, many people who originally planned to go to Argentina ended up in Uruguay instead.

European migration to Uruguay has changed through the years. Originally, under Spanish colonialism, only Spanish settlers were encouraged to move to the New World. After independence, however, the new government realized that many more people were needed to settle the interior and develop the country. From 1830 to 1870, there was a boom in European migration, with Spanish, French, and Italians making up large immigrant groups. In 1860 it was estimated that 48 percent of the population was foreign-born. Nearer the turn of the 20th century, Italians had become the largest group of new immigrants.

The last wave of European immigrants began arriving at the start of the century and did not subside until the 1930s. Most of those immigrants were Jews from parts of Europe where their religion was not tolerated. Some were Spanish and Portuguese Jews, but in the 1930s the majority were from Germany. Immigration has slowed down dramatically since the 1950s.

Once in Uruguay, most immigrants chose to live in and around Montevideo and other large urban centers. More than half of the total population lives in Montevideo and in the neighboring department of Canelones. The general

A crowded street in Montevideo. Most of the immigrant population is found in urban centers like Montevideo.

The slave trade had been in existence for some time when the Spanish crown made it legal in 1791. At that time, Montevideo was designated the official slave-trading port for the Río de la Plata area. Many ships came bringing Africans who had been taken forcefully from their homes and shipped as cargo to the New World to be sold. Despite their debased social position, slaves participated in all the major wars of the 19th century, including the independence movement when they fought with General José Artigas. The first step to end slavery came in 1825 when trading for new slaves was prohibited and all slaves born in Uruguay were given their freedom. There were other laws aimed at ending slavery, but it was not until 1853 that all African Uruguayans finally gained their freedom.

Aside from their loyal fighting alongside their white countrymen in all conflicts of the 19th century, African Uruguayans also contributed to the diverse Uruguayan culture.

pattern is that those born in small villages move to the capital city of their department to look for work, while those born in the department capitals tend to move to Montevideo. With so few people left to look after the countryside, Uruguay is almost a city-state.

As well as movement into and within the country, there has also been a steady pattern of emigration—residents leaving the country. This is a far more recent trend and one that has slowed down in recent times, but it has contributed to Uruguay's modern demographic problems. The emigration of the young and educated started when the country began to experience serious economic problems in the 1960s and continued during the military dictatorship in the 1970s. Although most went to Argentina, where they could blend in easily, the United States, Australia, Spain, Brazil, and Venezuela were also popular destinations. When Julio María Sanguinetti became the first democratically elected president in 1984, he invited all exiles and migrants back. Sadly, only a handful returned. Many who visited shortly after the election were so shocked by the poor state of the country that they decided never to return.

AN AGING POPULATION

Uruguay has an unusual demographic pattern. With the slowdown in immigration halfway through the 20th century and acceleration in emigration, Uruguay lost and could not replace its youth. The average age of the population increased as the arrival of young immigrants declined. It increased even more in the 1960s and 1970s when young people fled by the thousands to escape the country's repressive junta, or dictatorship. Another 100,000 young and highly qualified Uruguayans left during the country's lengthy and deep recession between 1995 and 2002 for greener pastures in Europe and the United States. That is a prominent reason why Uruguay has the highest proportion of elderly people in all South America.

Uruguay has the highest proportion of elderly citizens in all of South America.

Advances in medical science and availability of contraception has led to a reduction in the number of births in Uruguay, thus raising the average age of its people.

The trend was widened even more by changes in the birth and death rates in the 20th century. Advances in medicine made it possible for people to live longer, and the introduction of birth control methods made it possible for families to have fewer children. When both the birthrate and the death rate decrease, the average age of the population increases, as young people grow up and fewer children are born. By contrast, most other South American countries have the reverse problem of huge populations under the age of 15 due to high birth and low death rates. Uruguay is more like North American countries in its demographics than it is like its neighbors.

Eduardo Hughes Galeano has been a cultural envoy for his country, bringing the problems of Uruguay to the attention of the world through his writing.

SOCIAL CLASSES

Uruguay is unlike its neighbors in terms of its class system, too. Although there are rich people and poor people, the country has a large middle class. Roughly 5 percent of the population can be considered extremely wealthy, while about 50 percent would be considered working class, leaving 45 percent in the middle.

Class distinctions are not clear-cut, but generally, those at the top own lots of land or big businesses or control politics. Middle-class citizens own medium-sized farms or businesses, work for the government, teach, or are professionals such as doctors, dentists, and skilled technicians.

The lower class includes rural workers who own no land, farmers with small plots of land, and blue-collar and unskilled workers such as those who work in factories. The unemployed in both the cities and the countryside are also counted in the lower class.

Workers harvesting fruit at an orchard. Such laborers are considered to be in the lower class of Uruguayan society, performing most of the nation's manual work.

GALEANO: URUGUAY'S BEST-KNOWN WRITER

Eduardo Hughes Galeano was born in Montevideo in 1940. He started writing for a literary journal called Marcha, *which was well-known for its high quality of writing. He left the country during the repression to live in Spain. He returned in 1984 to become the editor of a new journal,* Brecha. *The military had shut down* Marcha.

His most famous book is Open Veins of Latin America, *a history of Latin America from the European conquest to 1971 (when the book was first published). It is a political commentary on how the people of Latin America have been used first by the Spanish and Portuguese and then by other more powerful nations. That pivotal book has been issued in over 30 editions and remains on reading lists in universities around the world. More recently, the widely read author wrote an interesting trilogy,* Memory of Fire, *published in 1988. It is a collection of stories, poems, newspaper articles, and reports detailing life in Latin America from before the European conquest to the present. It complements* Open Veins, *which is more of a straightforward history. Galeano's books, which are a unique blend of history, fiction, journalism, and political analysis, have been translated into more than 20 languages.*

Galeano has also written fiction. His most notable novel, Days and Nights of Love and War, *is about living in a military dictatorship, based on experiences in a repressive Uruguay.*

LIFESTYLE

A busy street in Uruguay.

THE LIFESTYLE OF URUGUAYANS IS greatly influenced by a significantly larger neighbor, Argentina. Minority ethnic groups have a lesser influence on Uruguayan culture.

NATIONAL CHARACTER AND DRESS

Most Uruguayans will describe themselves as cultured, generous, and conservative. They do not like to be ridiculed and tend to be cautious—they try never to rush into things. They are humble about themselves and are very family-oriented.

Uruguayans browsing through knickknacks at a Saturday flea market.

An Uruguayan man drinking maté that he made with the hot water in his thermos.

On the negative side, they themselves say they are frequently late. In fact, one humorist noted, "In Uruguay, nothing starts on time because if one is punctual, one is alone."

Uruguayans are also fiercely egalitarian—they prefer to make things equal for everyone. As this has been part of the general governmental design, before and after the dictatorship, it is no surprise that the national character reflects that.

Two passions that unite Uruguayans are soccer and maté, an herbal tea. It is said that, "Uruguayan males are born with a diploma in soccer under their arms." This is definitely their national sport. Maté for them is habitual, something like drinking coffee for many North Americans. People sip it throughout the day, and Uruguayans can often be seen carrying a thermos of hot water to use in making maté.

One feature of the Uruguayan character that stems from the indigenous past is called the Garra Charrúa (GAR-rah char-ROO-ah,), meaning Charrúan Talon (as of a bird of prey). *Garra Charrúa* refers to character traits of

Uruguayans look up to and admire the values of the gauchos.

persistence, fierceness, and bravery. When Uruguayans engage in sports, soccer in particular, they say they have the *Garra Charrúa*, recalling Charrúan Indian qualities of courage and fierceness.

There is no national dress or manner of dressing that distinguishes Uruguayans from any other people of European descent. About the only thing that sets apart urban Latin Americans from urban North Americans is that their Western dress codes are often slightly more formal in the south. Latin American women also tend to dress more often in skirts than in pants.

The only traditional dress one finds in Uruguay comes from the gauchos. The gaucho, or cowboy, heritage of Uruguay is very important and people work hard at preserving it.

RURAL AND URBAN CLASSES

THE RURAL CLASSES Historically, the interior of the country was settled slowly as people moved to the open grasslands to be closer to their cattle, sheep, and horses. Gradually, during the 19th century, fences were built to create large ranches, called estancias. The soil in the grasslands is not rich enough for intensive farming, so these estancias are used to pasture herds of animals. To run a ranch, only a few people are needed to make sure the fences are mended and the animals are healthy. There are a few class divisions among rural people, which results in some differences in lifestyle.

Ranch owners typically do not live on their isolated ranches. Those who own large plots of land—65,000 acres (26,305 ha) is not uncommon—are quite wealthy and prefer to live in Montevideo where their families have access to the best private schools and all other urban services. Even the important annual agricultural fair is held in Montevideo. Such ranching elites have traditionally supported the Blanco Party and in general are more conservative than urban elites. The large estancias are usually divided into sections for different uses—one for cattle, another for sheep, and one more for crops (usually animal feed), and each section

Gauchos herding cattle into a pen.

is managed by a foreman. The foremen are often related to the ranch owners. Under the foreman is the ranger, who is like a modern gaucho. The rangers, in turn, may supervise a few ranch hands, or helpers, who do the more ordinary tasks, like chores.

Far from the center, life in the countryside is much slower but is also much more hierarchical. Ranch owners or foremen are unlikely to socialize with their rangers or ranch hands, for example, and they would rarely permit a marriage across these divisions. Being more isolated from trends in the cities has also meant that rural workers tend to be more religious and are less likely to become members of labor unions.

Only those families who can afford to send their children to live in towns can guarantee that the teens will get a high school education. The poorest 5 percent of the population are the ranch hands, who make little money, and the owners of small farms, who cannot afford to travel to the city to take advantage of urban services.

Life in the country moves more slowly than in the cities, and is more serene.

THE URBAN CLASSES Class divisions are also found in the cities. At the top of the heap are the business and political elites. Those are the families that have historically controlled trade and government. The business and industrial elites during the 19th century were considered inferior to the landowning class. This changed during the 20th century, so now the big ranching and business families tend to intermarry and combine their interests. Together, they form the richest 5 percent of the population.

The political elite is composed of a small group of families that have traditionally sent their sons to law school to give them a strong base from which to enter politics. Nowadays, there are more political parties, and control of the government is not restricted to a few important families. There still are "political families," but in fact, the newer parties are being led by middle-class teachers, lawyers, and civil servants—and smart women, too.

Next down on the ladder is the urban middle class, which includes professionals, teachers, business managers, and owners of small businesses. They are not quite the majority of the population, but that group is definitely the one setting the standard in Uruguayan society.

As the economy worsened in the 1960s, middle-class women started joining the workforce to supplement their family income. That trend mirrors what happened in North America at the same time. One critical difference is that the middle class in Uruguay can often afford to hire female servants to help around the house, making it easier for Uruguayan women to work without having to work at home, too.

The proud owner of a small general store.

Construction workers are usually low on the income scale.

At the bottom of the income scale are the blue-collar workers and urban poor. Uruguay has never had a very large industrial workforce simply because its small size meant that there were never many industries. Those who do work in industry, however, have tended to maintain a reasonable standard of living with the help of the unions. All urban industries are unionized in Uruguay, and that has meant that workers have been well protected. Like middle-class women, working-class women have had to join the workforce if they can, but since they cannot afford domestic help, they often work twice as hard. Some working-class families have been unable to earn sufficient income in the usual way to survive. Over the last few years, there has been an increase in what is known as informal sector activities. Those are income-generating behaviors that are not reported to the government, either because people do not want to pay taxes or because they are illegal. Some examples of work in the informal sector are domestic work, trading in goods smuggled from Brazil, and piecework such as sewing or knitting at home.

Also included in the lowest income group are the unemployed and retired people who live only on government pensions.

The gaucho image still symbolizes a glorious past of freedom and self-reliance for modern Uruguayans. Gaucho traditions are celebrated during a special festival once a year.

Gaucho traditions and clothing date back to Spanish colonial times when there were no fences to mark property, thus cattle and sheep roamed freely. The first Spaniards to take advantage of such herds were a hardy group of expert horsemen who galloped across the plains, rounding up cattle and sheep as they rode. They lived on the land and camped out for days on end, far from the nearest shelter. Their main diet was beef cooked over open fires, washed down with maté. Those early gauchos were independent and tough men who cast an image of self-sufficiency that persists today.

Typical gaucho dress developed from the demands of rough outdoor living and long days of horseback riding. Gauchos always carried a large blanket with a hole in the middle that could double as a raincoat, poncho, or sleeping bag. They also wore something called a chiripá (chee-ree-PAH), which was a sort of skirt worn over the seat of the trousers to protect their pants from wear from the saddle. The gauchos' shirts and pants were always loose and baggy to permit free movement. They wore rastras (RAHS-trahs), or wide belts, made of leather with metal ornamentation—often gold or silver—and soft leather boots. The whole outfit was topped with a soft, brimmed hat of black felt.

Essential equipment for the gaucho included a horse and saddle, of course, a long knife called a façon (FAH-sone), and the bola, or boleadora (the projectile weapon of rocks and leather thongs used to bring down big animals).

In the 1870s wealthy people started buying pieces of land and fencing in the animals. Fences spelled the end of the gaucho era, since those fiercely independent men were forced to work for landowners—to work, moreover, in much more confined areas. Today there are still ranch hands on horseback, but their clothes have been modernized and their open-air way of life is no longer carefree and independent.

FAMILY LIFE AND GENDER ROLES

URUGUAYAN FAMILIES As in other Latin American countries, family ties are very strong. The ideal family model is both the nuclear and the extended family. A nuclear family is made up of the father and mother and their children. An extended family includes the grandparents, the adult children, and their spouses and children. The extended family is more likely to be found in rural areas, though recently there are more extended families doubling up in cities. That is because young married couples are finding it more and more difficult to afford their own apartment or house.

In the cities family size is quite small, the average being two children per couple. As the children grow up, they will live with their parents until they themselves are married. But it is not unusual for people in their thirties to continue to live at home because they are unmarried or cannot afford a place of their own.

A family enjoying a day at the beach. Both nuclear and extended family ties tend to be very strong and loving in Uruguay.

"There are no convincing reasons to limit women's education when the State invests considerable sums of money to expand the male education."—José Batlle y Ordóñez

COMPADRAZGO   One practice that has continued in the countryside is *compadrazgo* (cohm-pah-DRAHZ-go) or godparenthood. When a baby is baptized, the parents choose two godparents (a man and a woman, not necessarily married to each other) to help the child through various stages of its life. The usual pattern is for the new parents to choose godparents who are richer than they are.

The relationship between godchild and godparents is lifelong: godparents help their godchildren with schooling and finding a job, as well as helping them start families of their own. In return, the godchild will lend a hand to the godparents whenever asked and may even vote the way they vote as a display of loyalty. Those kinds of ties across class and family lines create a network of durable relationships that bind a community together.

Two classes of Uruguayans rarely go to university: the urban poor, who must start working young to supplement the family income; and rural families who cannot afford the living expenses of students away from home.

A self-employed Uruguayan woman tends to her stall at a Sunday market in Montevideo.

THE STRUGGLE FOR WOMEN'S RIGHTS

At the beginning of the 20th century Uruguayan women had very few rights. Their husbands were legally responsible for them and their property. If a woman were given money or land by her father, she lost control of it when she married. She also did not have the right to sue for divorce, although a husband might beat and even kill his wife if he caught her with another man. She could not vote and was treated basically as a child by the legal system. Women did not earn the same amount of money for work of comparable value and were expected to stay home and raise children.

José Batlle's reforms made some progress with divorce laws, but women themselves had to organize and fight for their rights. One outstanding woman who made a difference was Paulina Luisi. She was born in 1875 and became the first Uruguayan woman to get a medical degree. Throughout her life, she was committed to children's welfare and women's rights to education and to the vote. She represented Uruguay at a number of international conferences on women's and children's issues and was the first woman to serve as an official representative of her government at an intergovernmental conference in 1923. Along with other feminists, both male and female, Luisi managed to see women get the vote in 1938 for the first time. Finally, in 1946, the Law of Civil Rights of Women was passed, guaranteeing women equality with men. Dr. Luisi died in 1950, but she will always be remembered as an inspiration to women everywhere struggling for their rights.

WOMEN'S ROLES Women in Uruguay have had the benefit of legal protection and hard-won rights for much longer than their neighbors. There is still an expectation that men should be "macho"—that they will be the breadwinners and heads of their families. It is quite acceptable for women to work outside the home, but they are still responsible for child care and domestic tasks as well, including shopping, cleaning, and cooking.

Young girls, especially in the cities, are given the same educational opportunities as boys. In the countryside, poor families often cannot afford to send all their children to high school and will choose to educate the boys before girls, believing that their future chances for getting work will be greater. Girls from poorer families often migrate to towns or big cities to find work as live-in domestic servants.

EDUCATION

Uruguay was the first country in Latin America to have free, universal, and compulsory education. In 1877 the Law of Common Education was passed, making education available to all school-age children. Uruguay also has one of the best school systems and literacy rates in Latin America. Literacy is estimated at 98 percent, and there is no difference between men and women in this regard. Also, nearly 100 percent of school-age children attend elementary school. The first nine years of school are compulsory; children are required to attend school until they are 14 years old.

Schoolchildren in public schools do not have to wear uniforms, but they must wear smocks over their clothes. That depicts all children as equal, whether rich or poor. Public schools are free and secular. There are also private schools in the cities that cater to wealthy families.

There is one public university and five private universities in Montevideo. The University of the Republic is publicly supported and free to anyone who

The University of the Republic has long been acknowledged as a very good medical school. Although many programs there suffered under the military dictatorship, this public university continued to offer a high-quality degree in medicine to local and foreign students.

Uruguayan boys, dressed as required by their schools, pose for a photo.

has completed high school, although students do have to pay for books, and there are some small fees for the use of university facilities. Private universities such as the Catholic University charge tuition fees.

The average university program takes four to six years, but most students take longer to finish. There are discounts on public transportation for undergraduates and subsidized cafeterias with inexpensive food for all students. With a scarcity of jobs for graduates, there is little incentive to graduate quickly.

HEALTH

Health care, along with other social programs, is subsidized by the government. Subsidized care is not universal, however; those who can afford private health care are expected to pay for it. Uruguayans have adequate facilities nationwide for medical care. There are some 112 hospitals in Uruguay.

The average life expectancy in Uruguay is 72.89 years for men and 79.51 years for women; infant mortality is about 11.66 deaths per 1,000 births. Those numbers are not yet as good as in developed countries, but they are respectable by Latin American standards.

HOUSING

In the cities there are both apartment buildings and single family houses. On the outskirts are areas of suburban family homes. In the bigger cities, there is also public housing, which is subsidized by the government for low-income tenants.

In the countryside, being rich or poor makes a huge difference in how one lives. The poorest agricultural workers subsist in shantytowns of shoddily constructed shacks that do not have running water or sewage systems. By contrast, the rich live in sprawling ranch houses that were often built in the 19th century and modernized over time. They are normally big, one-storied buildings. The walls are solidly constructed, and the rooms are large enough to entertain many guests. Today some of those homes are open to tourists who want to see what life is like out in the open grasslands.

Ranches are usually separated by great distances, so when ranch owners and their families visited one another, they would often stay for days. For that reason, houses were built with extra bedrooms and big dining and living rooms.

RELIGION

The Cathedral of Montevideo is in the Old City area.

ALTHOUGH A HIGH PERCENTAGE OF citizens belong to the Roman Catholic Church, Uruguayan society is mostly secular, meaning that much of daily life is simply not religious.

According to the constitution, no religion is recognized as official or preferred. As a result, Christmas is officially called Family Day and Easter Week is known as Tourism Week, or Semana Criolla (Creole Week). Although most Uruguayans are not religious, they have always tolerated other faiths. Uruguay is quite exceptional in this regard in South America, where most people are practicing Catholics.

The San Fernando de Maldonado cathedral in Punta del Este was built in 1895.

Compared with citizens of other Latin American countries, Uruguayans are not as heavily influenced by Roman Catholicism. Uruguay is very tolerant of other faiths, and in fact, the right to religious freedom is spelled out in its constitution. Since its independence, there has been a decline in the importance and emphasis of Catholicism in both state and personal affairs.

77

A class in session. Religious instruction is banned from Uruguayan public schools.

A SECULAR SOCIETY

Compared with most of its neighbors in South America, Uruguay has been much less influenced by the Roman Catholic Church from colonial times to the present. Historically, Spain sent out conquistadores and priests together to take over Indian societies and convert them to Catholicism. Since Uruguay had few Indians—and those were very difficult to control—there was less opportunity for priests. Of course, the settlers built their own churches and continued to practice their religion, but the number of priests in Uruguay was always relatively small.

When Uruguay became independent and the first constitution was written, Catholicism was the official religion, but the constitution protected the people's right to religious freedom. As early as 1844, British traders living in Montevideo were allowed to build an Anglican church for themselves. That was one of the first Protestant churches raised in Spanish America. In 1935, when the English church was in the way of a new sea wall planned for the city, the government paid to have it moved stone by stone to another site, because it was considered a historical landmark.

Since independence, Uruguay has become more and more secularized and fewer events depend on church participation. For example, in 1837 civil marriages were made legal. In 1861 the state took over public cemeteries

Devotees of the African-American Umbandista cult present offerings to Lemanja, the African goddess of the sea, in Montevideo.

so that the Catholic Church could not prevent non-Catholics from being buried in them. During José Batlle's two terms as president (1903—07 and 1911—15), many more secular laws were enacted. Batlle believed that all religions should be tolerated equally and that none should control people's lives in a legal way. In 1907 he made divorce legal. In Catholicism, divorce is prohibited, and if two people want to end their marriage, they must get special permission from the Church. Many Catholics believe it is a sin to divorce. With its new law, the state gave permission to divorce to couples who wanted to end their marriage.

In 1909 all religious instruction was banned from public schools. The constitution created by Batlle and finally passed in 1919 officially separated church and state, and Catholicism was no longer the recognized religion of Uruguay.

A man praying in the Church of the Lord of Patience in Montevideo. Prayers are jotted on the walls behind him.

SOCIETY OF JESUS: THE JESUITS IN URUGUAY

The Society of Jesus was founded in 1540 in Europe. A Catholic born in Spain, Ignatius Loyola was alarmed by the Reformation, a period in the early 1500s when some Christians split away from the Roman Catholic Church and organized Protestant groups. He undertook to start a new religious order to encourage more men to remain loyal to the Catholic Church. Priests of this order call themselves Jesuits, and one of their primary goals is to convert non-Christian peoples to Catholicism. They are painstakingly trained in arts and sciences, so that they are capable and disciplined teachers as well as religious leaders.

Jesuits were very important in the earliest stages of settlement in South America. They were among the few Europeans brave enough to try to communicate with often hostile Indians. They also attempted to learn native languages and teach Indians how to speak Spanish. In Uruguay, Paraguay, and Argentina, the Jesuits built missions where the Indians could live and work under their protection. Sometimes these settlements, called reductions (reducciónes), were the only safe havens from death or slavery for the converted Indians.

Events in Europe in the 1700s ended the Jesuit presence in the New World. Other Catholic religious orders and some of the European royal courts were very jealous of the power of Jesuits around the world. In 1767 Charles III of Spain was convinced by others to banish the Jesuits from all Spanish territory. That was a sad time for the Indians living in the reductions. Many of them were taken by European settlers to be virtual slaves on their farms. Others tried to turn back to their old way of life, but were not successful. An intriguing question is, Would there still be a native population in Uruguay if the Jesuits had stayed?

ROMAN CATHOLICS

There are many conflicting statistics about how many people call themselves Roman Catholic and how many people actually follow the dogma of the Church. About 47.1 percent of the Uruguayan population identify themselves as Catholic. Most Catholic babies are still baptized, but in the capital it is estimated that only about 10 percent of baptized Catholics go to mass on Sunday. Although religion has minimal impact on public life, Uruguayans do normally participate in religious festivals and rituals. Generally, church attendance is higher in rural areas than in the cities and is higher among women than among men. Protestants make up 11.1 percent of the population, nondenominational Christians make up 23.2 percent, 0.3 percent are Jewish, and 18.3 percent do not adhere to any particular religion or believe in other faiths.

OTHER RELIGIONS

PROTESTANTS There have been Protestants in Uruguay since at least 1844 when the Anglican church was built. During the 20th century many other Protestant churches were established in Uruguay, part of the larger trend of Protestantization in Catholic South America. Many American evangelical

Protestants at an evangelical rally in Uruguay.

FOLK BELIEFS

In many South American societies, folk beliefs come from indigenous cultures. The new settlers taught their religion to the natives and in exchange learned about their beliefs and superstitions. With such a small original indigenous population, Uruguayans did not have much opportunity to learn from those original inhabitants. So such folk tradition that does exist in Uruguay comes largely from the time when many Uruguayan men were gauchos roughing it in the open plains.

One folk belief inspired from this gaucho era is that one should never kill fireflies. These flickering insects are thought to keep the spirits of the dead company at night with their little lamps. Another rural superstition is that a son born seventh in line will periodically turn into an animal such as a wolf, pig, or goat. He is called Lobizón (oh-bee-SON), from lobo, wolf. This is similar to the European werewolf superstition that the full moon makes those who have been bitten by a wolf turn into a mutant creature, half-man and half-wolf.

churches set up in Uruguay since the 1960s and have been hard at work to convert Catholics to Protestantism. Since Uruguayans are not very religious to start with, the new missionaries have managed to attract only small congregations.

Some of the Protestant churches represented in Uruguay include Baptists, Seventh-day Adventists, Methodists, and the Evangelical Mennonite Church. Altogether, they account for approximately 11.1 percent of the population.

JEWS Before the repression and dictatorship there was a sizable Jewish community in Montevideo. There were six active synagogues with large congregations. Today only 0.3 percent of the total population are Jews.

Jews had migrated to Uruguay because it was known to have a religiously tolerant society. The first large wave of European Jewish immigrants came at the beginning of the 20th century. The second wave of mostly German Jews arrived in the 1930s when the Nazis were beginning to persecute the Jews in Germany. Many Uruguayan Jews left Uruguay during the repression in the 1970s, so now they are only a tiny fraction of the society.

LANGUAGE

Men reading newspapers clipped onto a stand.

A

T THE SIMPLEST LEVEL, ALL Uruguayans are Spanish-speaking. The full story, however, is far more complex and interesting. Uruguayans speak a variety of Spanish and colorful dialects that were created through a blending of other languages.

SPANISH IN THE NEW WORLD

The language spoken in Uruguay and most of the rest of South America is Spanish, with the notable exception of Brazil, where Portuguese is

As with most of South America, Uruguay's national language is Spanish. Historical influences from other languages, however, such as Italian, led to the development of peculiarities in Uruguayan Spanish. Uruguayan Spanish is also influenced by Portuguese, spoken by its Brazilian neighbor. The language also differs between regions.

Uruguayans browsing through crates of books at a street stall.

spoken. That fact is taken for granted today because it is well known that the first foreign settlers of the continent were from Spain.

Many languages were spoken in Spain way back when settlers were first arriving in South America. To list some examples, in the 15th and 16th centuries such languages as Castilian, Catalan, Asturian, Leonese, Aragonese, Basque, and Galician were all spoken in different regions of the country. Castilian , Catalan, Galician, and Basque are four that have survived into the 21st century and can be heard spoken today.

Why did a particular language spoken in only some parts of Spain become the single dominant language in all of Spain's New World colonies? The answer is that migration to the New World followed a specific pattern.

An advertisement in Spanish of a movie from the United States.

All settlement in the New World from Spain was planned in the province of Castile in central Spain, so that those applying for consent to leave Spain had to have learned enough Castilian to make an application. Those chosen were sent to either Andalusia or Seville to wait for a boat to take them across the Atlantic Ocean. The waiting often took as much as a year, during which time the emigrants learned the local language.

In addition, ships' crews were all from Andalusia or the Canary Islands, which had become a province of Spain in the late 1400s. Since crossing the ocean took such a long time, ships had to stop in the Canary Islands to reprovision. All New World settlers followed that route, so most of them came to speak a common language by the time they arrived in their new homes. The fact that Castilian and Andalusian are quite similar reinforced the trend toward a common language. At the same time, Castilian Spanish became increasingly more common throughout all of Spain because it was the language of the king and his court. So after five centuries, people in Latin America and in Spain both speak a language that is quite similar but not exactly the same.

The Spanish spoken in Latin America has been influenced by such other agents as time and distance. Those factors led to differences in pronunciation and word usage. Hence, the Spanish of the New World settled by the Spanish is not exactly the same as the language that came to dominate modern Spain.

Some of the differences in vocabularies between modern Spain and Latin America can be traced to the time the settlers spent in port towns or on board ships. Many words that are used every day in Latin America are used only on board ships in Spain.

Latin America	Spain	English Translation
botar	*tirar*	to throw out
amarrar	*atar*	to tie up
balde	*cubo*	bucket
timón	*volante*	steering wheel

Although most of the original populations were killed off early in Uruguay's history, there are some remnants of their languages on the map of Uruguay. Río Yi was named by the Charrúas—the tribe that was traitorously massacred—who also used the boleadora, *or bola, the weapon of leather thongs and rocks used to entangle animals. This was adopted by the gauchos and is still called by its Charrúan name.*

Place names such as Paysandú and Yaguarí come from the language of the Guaraní. Since those populations—the Charrúas and the Guaraní—were very small and did not mix for long with Spanish speakers, there are no obvious influences on Uruguayan Spanish other than these few words.

Other words in Latin American Spanish are from a very old form of the language and are no longer used at all in European Spanish. Some examples of those are *lindo* (beautiful), *cobija* (blanket), and *pollera* (skirt).

THE SPANISH OF URUGUAY

The official language of Uruguay is Spanish, but the reality of what people speak in daily life and why they speak that way is more complex. In Uruguay, as in any other country, there are historical influences from other languages and other times.

Most of the immigrants from Spain came from Castile, Andalusia, Galicia, and the Canary Islands, and they all took the peculiarities of their local Spanish with them. An example is the Canary usage of *pibe/piba* for guy/gal. These words are not commonly heard outside Uruguay and Argentina.

There were also a significant number of Italian immigrants to the Río de la Plata area in the first half of the 20th century. They used their own language for a while before becoming fluent in Spanish. One of the words that has entered Uruguayan Spanish from Italian is *chau* (*ciao* in Italian), which means good-bye.

Uruguay's location between Argentina and Brazil, and the fact that it was a province of Brazil briefly in the 19th century, tells us that there is also a

A SIMPLE GUIDE TO SPANISH PRONUNCIATION

Spanish is one of the easiest languages to learn because what you read is what you say, as long as you know the rules of pronunciation. The Spanish alphabet has 3 extra consonants. The alphabet looks like this:

a b c ch d e f g h i j k l ll m n ñ o p q r s t u v w x y z

There are 5 main vowel sounds:

a	=	ah	=	*like the* a *in cat, so* alma *(soul) is AHL-mah*
e	=	ay	=	*like the* ay *in day, so* mente *(mind) is MAYN-tay*
i	=	ee	=	*like the* ee *in teeth, so* infinitud *(infinity) is een-feen-ee-TOOD*
o	=	oh	=	*like the* o *in bone, so* poco *(little) is POH-koh*
u	=	oo	=	*like the sound in chew or zoo, so* una *(a) is OO-nah*

Sometimes there are combinations of vowels, for example ia or ue. Just make each vowel sound separately. So ia becomes ee-ah and ue becomes oo-ay.

Most Spanish consonants are the same as English ones, but there are a few differences:

ch	=	*same as the English sound in church, so* che *(term of address) is chay*
ll	=	*same sound as* l + y *in English, so* calle *(street) is cahl-ye*
ñ	=	*same sound as* n + y *in English, so* mañana *(morning, tomorrow) is pronounced man-yan-ah*
h	=	*always silent, so* hambre *(hunger) is AM-bray*
j	=	*like the English* h *in hat, so* pájaro *(bird) is PAH-ha-row*
qu	=	*like the English* k *in keep, so* pequeño *(small) is pay-KAYN-yo*
v	=	*like the English* b, *but a little softer*
x	=	*like the English* s *except when it is between two vowels, then it is an h sound, so* oxicanto *is oh-hee-CAN-toh*

(continued)

y = like the English s, as in mission

z = like the English s in so, so azul *(blue)* is AH-sool

The letters *c* and *g* are tricky because they each have two pronunciations:

c with e *or* i *has an* s *sound, so* lúcida *(lucid or clear) is LOO-see-dah; but* c *with* a, o, *or* u *is hard, like* k, *so* buscar *(to look for) is BOOS-kar*

g with e *or* i *has an* h *sound, but* g *with* a, o, *or* u *is hard, like the English* g *in* gut, *so* frágil *(fragile) is FRAH-heel, but* siga *(I follow) is SEE-gah*

Portuguese influence in Uruguayan Spanish. There is even a whole separate language that combines Spanish and Portuguese and is spoken only along the Brazil-Uruguay border.

Although Uruguay is not a big or populous country compared with its neighbors, it is big enough to have regional variations in language. The majority of the population lives in Montevideo where the dialect is virtually the same as that in Buenos Aires, Argentina. This dialect is called Porteño (por-TAYN-yoh) and is very distinctive. Part of the vocabulary of Porteño comes from a working-class slang called Lunfardo (loon-FAR-doh). The special words used by poorer people came to be used by the population as a whole through the lyrics of popular music, especially the pervasive tango music.

In the interior of the country, people speak a couple of different dialects. The most notable is Fronterizo (fron-tayr-EE-zoh), which is spoken close to the Brazilian frontier in the north. Fronterizo (also called Portuñol and Bayano) combines features of Spanish and Portuguese and is considered to be a third language. Uruguayans have learned this language because for some time there have been better educational facilities and employment opportunities in Brazil than in Uruguay. The populations living along the border have socialized and lived together for many years; this combination language is the result.

Two types of speech that have passed out of use are Cocoliche (ko-ko-LEE-chay) and the gaucho language. Those once vibrant dialects were spoken

For a period in the 18th and 19th centuries, Montevideo was the main port for the trade in African slaves. Some words from African languages are still used: *mucama* means a female domestic servant, and *candombe* (can-DOME-bey) is an African-based carnival ritual and dance.

Cocoliche was a version of Spanish spoken by Italian immigrants in the early part of the 20th century. When the first Italian immigrants were trying to learn Spanish, they found it easier at first to combine the language of their new country with their native tongue, mixing vocabulary and grammatical forms to create a very distinctive dialect. The second generation grew up learning fluent Spanish in the schools, and Cocoliche faded away.

Gaucho speech, a rural variety of language, preserves older words and forms of grammar. To a Spanish-speaking person, gaucho speech today might sound something like Shakespearean English to an American. Gaucho speech is associated with the lifestyle of those legendary men who roamed the open grasslands, herding wild cattle and horses. The idiom is preserved in early poetry and novels, but today, a real gaucho is very rare and so, too, is his particular variety of Spanish.

by particular groups in Uruguayan society. Because those groups no longer exist, the languages they spoke have also disappeared from daily life, but they have an afterlife in poetry and the theater.

Uruguayans value their beach time, like this woman reading a book on the beach.

ACCENT MARKS

The other thing needed to know to pronounce Spanish perfectly is how to read accent marks. You may have noticed that some words have little marks above a vowel. Unlike in some other languages (French, for example), these marks do not change the way the vowel is pronounced, but they do change the stress in the word. That means they point out which part of a word is to be said the strongest.

The general rule of stress in Spanish is that if there are two or more syllables (separate sounds), then the second to last one is stressed. Sometimes, however, this is not true, so stress marks tell the reader that the stress is different in that word. For example, the words frágil *and* pájaro *have stress marks to show where the stress should be made in these words. Frágil is FRAH-heel , with the emphasis on the first syllable of the word. Pájaro is PAH-hah-row, not pah-HAH-row as it would be pronounced if it had no stress marks.*

This all sounds very complicated, but once you practice a little, you will find Spanish is very easy to speak and musical to listen to. Here is a poem by one of Uruguay's most famous poets, Juana de Ibarbourou, about a palm tree. Using the rules above, practice saying the lines from her poem.

"Soneto a Una Palma"

Ya sin hambre ni sed, apenas alma
Apenas cuerpo que se va durmiendo;
Toda lúcida mente es como entiendo
La Infinitud de Dios en esta palma.

Cuando todo se vuelva eterna calma
Y siga el mar la frágil tierra hendiendo
Poco a poco mi espíritu, volviendo
Irá a buscar morada en esta palma

Tal vez pequeño pájaro de canto

O humilde y tierno ramo de oxicanto

Con una flor azul junto a su planta

Mi palma ya será me patria eterna

Y ha de tener por siempre una lucerna:

La luz de una amistad que siembra y canta.

"Sonnet to a Palm"

Without hunger or thirst, hardly a soul

Hardly a body that goes to sleep;

All lucid mind is how I understand

The Infinity of God in this palm.

When all returns to the eternal calm

And the sea returns to flood the fragile earth

Little by little my spirit, returning

Will go to look for shelter in this palm

Maybe as a small bird of song

Or humble and tender branch of morning glory

With a blue flower next to its plant

My palm will be my eternal homeland

And there always has to be a grand light:

The light of a friendship that plants and sings.

ARTS

An artist at work at the pedestrian mall, Peatonal Sarandi, in Montevideo.

URUGUAY HAS A SIGNIFICANT AND fruitful artistic community. With a historically high level of education and popular support for the arts, many types of creative expression have flourished in the tiny diamond-shaped republic. Uruguay has produced world-renowned painters, writers, and composers.

PERFORMING ARTS

Performing arts include music, theater, and dance. As a largely urban people, Uruguayans have a splendid and varied tradition of performing arts. Most of this vitality is centered in Montevideo, but department capitals and larger towns often support local theaters and performing musicians.

THEATER The Teatro Solís (Solís Theater) in Montevideo is the home of the National Comedy Repertory Company. This group of actors and directors regularly performs new and classic works by Latin American playwrights.

The most famous of Uruguayan playwrights is Florencio Sánchez. Born in 1875, he wrote plays set in the Río de la Plata region. His characters are usually Uruguayan, Argentinian, or Paraguayan and tend to represent the working class. His plays are famous for their realistic dialogue and insightful portrayal of life in the slums of Buenos Aires or

Uruguay has a rich artistic tradition. Theatergoing is a popular activity, and Uruguay has a number of theaters and acting companies that stage performances ranging from locally produced plays to Shakespeare. It is hard to escape music and dance in Uruguay, especially the tango and *candombe*. Uruguay has also produced a number of prolific visual artists and writers.

Montevideo. Some of his plays examine the conflicts arising between rural lifestyles and the modern changes introduced by the cities. Sánchez has been compared with famous Russian authors such as Dostoevsky and Gorky, who dealt with social confrontations.

Literary figures such as Pedro Figari, José Enrique Rodó, and Mario Benedetti are internationally acclaimed. A notable modern playwright is Mauricio Rosencof. He began writing in the 1960s but then decided to join the Tupamaros in their fight against the government. He was arrested and jailed for more than 10 years. Whenever he was allowed to have paper, he continued to write poetry in jail, mostly about what it feels like to be tortured and imprisoned. He was released in 1985 along with other Tupamaros.

Other theaters in Montevideo include the Odeón, which features productions of Shakespeare's plays along with modern dramas, and the Verdi, which produces mostly comedies. Universities and many secondary

The Teatro Solís in Montevideo has been beautifully renovated.

schools around the country support amateur theater groups. Uruguay also has a highly regarded independent theater movement that served as an outlet through which Uruguayans were able to express themselves politically, especially during the sixties.

DANCE AND MUSIC Perhaps the best-known music from this part of the world is the tango. The tango is most often associated with Buenos Aires, but Buenos Aires and Montevideo are culturally almost indistinguishable, and the tango developed in both places. The tango originated in the poor slums on the outskirts of Buenos Aires in the 1880s. It is both a type of dance and a special kind of music. A standard tango band has to include six players: two *bandoneons* (ban-doh-NAY-ons, a type of accordion made in Germany), two violins, a piano, and a double bass. At first the tango was only music and a style of intimate dance for men and women. Then in the

Uruguayans dancing the tango, an intimate, expressive music.

early 1900s, the lyrics became just as important as the music and the dance. The lyrics tended to have sad themes such as break-ups between lovers and street-life issues of the poor. Tango clubs opened all over Montevideo and Buenos Aires, and artists made a living by selling records and giving live performances. The most famous tango ever, "La Cumparsita," was written by a Uruguayan artist, Gerardo H. Matos Rodríguez (1897—1948).

Another popular art form is the *candombe*, which originated in the African-Uruguayan community. *Candombe* refers to both the music and the dance. The music is distinctive as it uses special African drums called *tamboriles* (tahm-BOR-eel-ehs). *Candombe* music and dance are part of two festivals celebrated in Montevideo.

Uruguay has produced two classical composers: Eduardo Fabini (1882—1950) and Héctor Errecart (1923—). Fabini is famous for his symphonies, while Errecart adapted traditional gaucho music to a classical form. His use of folk music themes has earned him world renown.

Uruguayans have always prized the right to free speech and open discussion of social and political problems. That unshakable tradition is nowhere more obvious than in the many forms of music that reflected popular opinion during the 19th and 20th centuries—and is already at work in the 21st century.

Young Uruguayan boys playing drums during a festival *con mucho gusto*!

Since the early days of independence, songwriters have told stories about the civil wars between the Colorados and the Blancos and have poked fun at their enemies in their songs. In more recent times, three performing art forms featuring songs have become the favored media for political observation: Carnival murgas *(MOOR-gahs), the tango, and the* canto popular *(KAHN-toh poh-poo-LAHR).*

Murgas *are written to be sung as part of street theater productions that take place in every neighborhood during Carnival (Mardi Gras). Those catchy songs frequently focus on some politician or political event from the past year.* Murgas *also refers to the bands that perform them.*

Tango songs are usually about the conflicts between men and women, especially of the lower classes. While singing about relationships, they also describe the life of the urban poor and new immigrants. In that sense, the tango becomes social commentary about life on the seedy streets.

Canto popular (popular song) started in the late 1960s when young musicians all over Latin America began to write songs about social problems and politics. They criticized their countries' governments and wanted to see changes in their countries. In Uruguay, canto popular *was heavily censored by the military, and many musicians were arrested or forced to leave the country. Some continued to try to make their messages heard through informal concerts and underground recordings. They were saluted as the only voice of the people under the systems of repression imposed by the army and police.*

VISUAL ARTS

Uruguay has a long tradition of supporting the visual arts and has produced some important artists. One of the most famous is the post-impressionist painter Pedro Figari (1861—1938), who gained international recognition for his works. Another artist who tried to capture rural living in his work is Carlos González. He is not a painter, however; rather, he makes prints called woodcuts, using woodblocks. They are made by carving a picture into blocks of wood, then inking the wood and pressing them onto paper. A separate block is made for each color. González's work portrays old-fashioned country life and focuses especially on gaucho culture. Many of his woodcuts depict gauchos in typical scenes: huddled over a campfire for warmth at night or sharing some maté on the plains. González's style is called primitivism because he uses very simple lines and carves only with a knife, making his work appear a little rough, much like his subjects.

The 19th century painter Juan Manuel Blanes (1830—1901) is one of Uruguay's most celebrated artists. He is well-known for his paintings of historical events, such as the painting *Oriental 33*. Another prominent artist was Joaquín Torres García (1874—1949), who was very active in the modern art community in Europe.

In Montevideo's parks, examples of Uruguayan sculpture can be seen. Perhaps the most photographed of all is the sculpture of the covered wagon or *carreta* (car-RAY-tah) being pulled by three oxen and driven by a bearded man. That well-known work represents the pioneers who first left the shores

La Carreta, part of a sculpture in Montevideo by José Belloni honoring the first pioneers.

Pedro Figari was born in Montevideo in 1861. He had no formal art training as a boy, though in 1886 he did sail to Venice to study with an artist there named Godofredo Sommavila. His real career as a painter did not start until 1921, when he was 60 years old and had his first exhibition in Buenos Aires.

Figari's favorite themes were scenes of rural life showing gauchos, African Uruguayans, country women, landscapes, and horses. His work is praised for his use of brush strokes and color to portray movement and light. Figari's landscapes are among the few that capture the special light of sunset on the open grasslands. In his work, he tried to retrieve life in the countryside in the 19th century as he remembered it. He also wanted to show that African Uruguayans had made important contributions to Uruguayan life. Some of his more widely known works feature scenes of candombes *(African-Uruguayan music and dance) and parties.*

In 1925 Figari moved to Paris, where he lived for the next 12 years, perfecting his painting style. In 1930 he won two awards for his art, one from Uruguay and another in Seville, Spain, at an international competition. He was a founding member of Uruguay's School of Arts and was also a member of the Friends of Art in Buenos Aires. Though his painting career was late to start and short-lived (he died in 1938), Pedro Figari produced over 3,000 paintings—a great many of them images of the 19th-century countryside that remain to remind Uruguayans of their rustic heritage.

of the Río de la Plata to settle the interior of the country. The sculpture is by José Belloni (1882—1965) and stands in Batlle and Ordoñez Park.

Another very famous sculpture is the gaucho on his horse that stands at the intersection of two large streets in downtown Montevideo. That much-photographed piece was made by José Luis Zorrilla de San Martín (1891—1975), son of a famous writer.

LITERARY ARTS

Literature is the area of artistic endeavor in which Uruguay has most excelled. As a result of a high literacy rate and a commitment to freedom

of speech, Uruguayans have turned more often to writing to express themselves than to any other art form. Many early works focused on nationalistic themes and on the rural heritage of the country.

Juan Zorrilla de San Martín (1855–1931), father of sculptor José Luis, was both a poet and a diplomat. In 1879 he wrote the poem "*La leyenda pátria*" ("*The Patriotic Legend*") in tribute to Uruguay's history. His other famous poem is the epic *Tabaré*, a long adventure story about Charrúa Indians. It is read throughout southern Latin America. Zorrilla also started a public newspaper in 1878 and served as Uruguay's ambassador to the Vatican, France, and Spain.

Javier de Viana (1868–1926) wrote about the end of the gaucho era. He captured the poverty and tragedy of gaucho life in his novel *Gaucha*. He has been compared to the famous 19th-century French writer Émile Zola, who also wrote about downtrodden people. Eduardo Acevedo Díaz (1851–1921) also portrayed gaucho life in his book *Soledad* (*Solitude*), published in 1894, but with a more upbeat tone.

Luis Carlos Benvenuto is a historian whose work makes Uruguay's history understandable to everyone. His *Brief History of Uruguay*, published in the 1960s, examines how and why Uruguay once had been rich but had stopped using its resources wisely. José Pedro Barrán (1934–) is another one of Uruguay's most important contemporary historians.

A newsstand selling popular news dailies, bringing readers a diverse choice of opinions.

SHAKESPEARE IN URUGUAY

Probably the most influential book ever written by an Uruguayan is Ariel *by José Enrique Rodó (1872—1917). Written in 1900 when Rodó was only 29, the book is actually a speech given by a fictitious teacher to his students. The students call the teacher Prospero because he keeps a big statue of Ariel in his study.*

Prospero and Ariel are characters from William Shakespeare's play The Tempest. *In* The Tempest, *the main character is a magician, Prospero, who lives alone on an island with his daughter and a savage, Caliban. Prospero's magic comes from a beautiful spirit he controls named Ariel. Ariel represents light and virtue, whereas Caliban represents greed and elemental impulses. Shakespeare's play serves as the framework used by the lecturing teacher to admonish his students how they should live their lives. He tells them they should try to develop all their human qualities, not just the ones that satisfy basic needs such as hunger and thirst. In other words, they should try to be more like Ariel than Caliban.*

Rodó's book suggested that the U.S. model of development was materialistic, like Caliban, whereas Latin American development should be idealistic, like Ariel. This was one of the most significant early efforts by Latin American thinkers to define the differences between South and North American values.

Another nonfiction writer, Carlos Maggi (1922—), is a humorist who likes to poke fun at Uruguayan culture and history. He especially derides Uruguayans who worship the gaucho past and the legends of the tango era. He has also written a screenplay, *The Yellow Ray*, a prizewinner at the International Film Festival at Brussels.

Before military censorship shut down many newspapers and magazines, Uruguay had a thriving tradition of literary criticism. The monthly magazine *Marcha* was read far beyond Montevideo because of its high standards of writing and criticism. Many young writers, including Eduardo Galeano (1940—), got their start by publishing stories in *Marcha*.

The military closed *Marcha* because it was too left-wing. Since 1985, another journal, *Brecha*, has been published. It is good but not as good as its predecessor because so many talented writers and editors have left the

JUANA DE AMERICA

Juana de Ibarbourou is Uruguay's best-loved female poet. She was born in Melo in 1892 and started publishing her poetry in 1918 when she moved to Montevideo. In her early life, she wrote and published plentifully and became very popular both within and outside of Uruguay. In 1929 she was nicknamed Juana de America (Juana of America) in a public ceremony in her honor at the University of the Republic.

Throughout her life, she faced many tragedies, including the deaths of her parents and of her husband. Those events are reflected in her poetry, which is sometimes very sad and religious. The theme of death is part of her "Sonnet to a Palm" found earlier in this book. A palm tree in Montevideo was dedicated to her in recognition of her beloved poetry. It was planted in the same spot as the original palm tree that she could see from her house and had inspired her sonnet.

In 1947 she was elected to the Academy of Fine Arts. In 1957 she was honored by UNESCO in a special meeting in her honor. Her works have all been reprinted many times and some have been translated into English. Sadly, she died poor and nearly forgotten in Montevideo in 1979. Once she died, the public remembered her contributions to Uruguayan art, and ironically, she was given a state funeral complete with the national flag on her coffin.

The beginning of the literary explosion in Uruguay came at the end of the 19th century. As open conflict between political factions declined, people began to consider what it meant to be Uruguayan.

country. Likewise with newspapers—many were forced to close during the dictatorship but have since reopened. With the return to its stable democracy, there are sure to be many more generations of amazing Uruguayan writers.

Most dailies are each associated with a particular political group and report the news according to their way of looking at things. No single newspaper is totally objective, but since everyone has access to more than one newspaper, any reader can easily get a balanced view by reading different opinions. The most widely circulated national newspaper is the *El País*.

FOLK CULTURE

Folk culture or folk art refers to the culture and art of the common people. Into this category falls much of the people's art of rural Uruguay. One particularly special type of folk craft is the maté cup and straw. Traditionally, maté was drunk from a hollowed-out gourd that was often decorated with silver and had silver around the rim. To drink out of the gourd, a silver straw called a *bombilla* (bohm-BEE-ya) was used. The set was usually carved in beautiful patterns, and it would have been among the prized possessions of any Uruguayan well off enough to afford it. Nowadays, those items have mostly been replaced with cheaper cups and straws, but older examples can be seen proudly displayed in many homes.

A more modern form of craft is the hand-knit sweater. Those bright and colorful garments are made by women working in their homes. They are thick and warm, and each one is unique. Knitting is an important source of income for poorer women in the countryside and the cities alike.

The maté cup is a form of Uruguayan folk art, nowadays often mass produced.

LEISURE

Two men sitting in the shade, enjoying a quiet afternoon.

A
GREAT NUMBER OF THINGS TO DO are available for Uruguayans to enjoy in their leisure time. They participate in many different sports and pastimes. Some of their free time is spent in ways similar to recreation in other countries, while some is spent in distinctly Uruguayan fashion.

SPORTS

SOCCER The most popular sport in the country is soccer, called *fútbol* in South America. Every able-bodied boy in Uruguay has played soccer

Youths playing soccer, one of the most popular games in Uruguay.

Uruguayans enjoy a wide variety of indoor and outdoor leisure activities. They also have a deep-seated passion for playing and watching soccer. Other popular sports are swimming, cycling, and tennis. In the summer, many people take to the water to windsurf or swim. Uruguayans also enjoy going to the movies and cafés, or shopping. They also like to take short vacations.

at school or in local fields, and everyone follows his favorite team. On July 13, 1930, the first World Cup soccer finals were held in Montevideo's Centenary Stadium, and Uruguay was one of the competing national teams. Uruguay won the championship, and the celebrations that resulted from that World Cup win are remembered still as the loudest and wildest in the history of the country.

In 1950 the Uruguay national team executed a major upset against heavyweight Brazil, which was favored to win the World Cup that year. The 2—1 victory over Brazil eventually became known as the *Maracanzo,* or the *Maracaná* Blow, as the match was played at the Maracaná stadium in Rio de Janeiro in Brazil.

OTHER SPORTS AND COMPETITIONS With so many good beaches lining the Río de la Plata between Montevideo and Punta del Este, water sports are

The Uruguayan national soccer team that triumphed over Brazil in 1950.

AGAINST THE ODDS

A Uruguayan airplane slammed into the Andes on October 13, 1972, killing 12 of the 45 passengers on board. Only 16 of the remaining people survived—19- to 33-year-old members of a rugby team. Their weekend game in Santiago, Chile, turned into an ordeal that lasted for 72 days. One by one the people who had survived the initial plane crash died from injuries or starvation. The team members endured extremely cold temperatures and starvation only to hear from their radio reception that the rescue parties had given up the search for them. In life-or-death desperation they reluctantly resorted to eating the flesh of the dead in order to survive. The true story inspired many books and the movie Alive, *starring Ethan Hawke.* National Geographic *also published an article about a team that re-created the brutally hard trek to find help by two of the young men to show what a tough journey it was even for trained people with proper equipment. In 2007 a documentary film entitled* Stranded: I've Come From a Plane That Crashed on the Mountains, *directed by Uruguayan Gonzalo Arijon, recounts one of the best-known 20th century tales of resilience and survival. After so many years, the survivors who were once labeled cannibals by their own countrymen, finally agreed to talk on camera with startling details, telling what their thoughts about it are today.*

very common in Uruguay. There are many boat races, both for motorboats and sailboats. Uruguay was once a stopover on one of the world's most prestigious races, the Volvo Ocean Race (formerly known as the Whitbread Round the World Race). During the summer, windsurfing competitions attract international competitors. Swimming is very popular, both as a competitive sport and as recreation. Every year there is a swimming race in the Punta del Este area, east of Montevideo.

Another race that attracts local and international attention is the annual Grand Prix auto race, also in Punta del Este. For people with more pedestrian interests, there is the San Fernando Marathon for runners. Besides water sports, Uruguayans enjoy basketball, tennis, polo, and golf. There are also competitions to show purebred Arabian horses, magnificent animals that are the pride of Uruguay.

CYCLING A popular leisure activity in Uruguay is cycling. There are numerous cycling clubs in Uruguay that compete both nationally and internationally. The governing body over cycling races in Uruguay is the Uruguayan Cycling Federation that successfully organized the Road and Track Pan-American Championships in Montevideo in 2008. The country's major cycling competition is the Tour de Uruguay. Many visitors to Uruguay opt to tour the nation on bicycles, rewarding them with intimate glimpses of the land and countrymen of the gauchos.

LEISURE ACTIVITIES

MOVIES AND THEATER One of the most popular forms of entertainment is the cinema. There are movie theaters all over the country. A small local film industry and foreign films provide entertainment variety. In larger urban centers, there is often a lively theater scene. In Montevideo, the population is worldly enough to attract touring international shows.

NIGHTLIFE Nightlife includes visiting *peñas* (PAYN-yahs), or clubs with live music. While the *peñas* tend to be most popular with the young, older people are more likely to go to old-fashioned tango bars to hear live music. For those with a sense of adventure, there are also clubs specializing in *candombe*, or African-Uruguayan music. Other musical tastes are served by symphony concerts and the occasional opera in Montevideo.

For people on limited budgets, nightlife might include a stroll around the downtown area and a stop in one of Montevideo's many cafés and late-night restaurants. Other types of recreation include gambling at one of the two government-owned casinos in Montevideo, Casino del Parque Rodó and the Hotel Carrasco Casino.

STROLLING Part of the Spanish heritage in Uruguayan culture is a love of strolling. It may not sound like much in the way of entertainment, but there is a long-standing tradition of going for walks with family and friends. In addition to shopping districts, Montevideo has many public parks and gardens well suited to this purpose. A place popular with young people is the Rambla, a road that runs parallel to Montevideo's waterfront. Ideally, a leisurely stroll leads to a coffee, ice cream, or maté with friends.

SHOPPING   Window shopping is also very popular. The main shopping street in Montevideo is 18th of July Avenue, which includes classy boutiques from all over the world. Recently, Montevideo has also promoted North American-style shopping malls, and several have sprung up in the city. Two are architecturally quite distinctive: Punta Carretas, a renovated prison, and Barrio Reus, located in a formerly impoverished area of the city. Architectural students renovated that dingy area by painting all the old tenement buildings in bright colors, turning it into a tourist attraction today.

On the weekends there are street markets or *ferías* (fay-REE-ahs), which sell everything from junk to priceless antiques. Food items such as vegetables and sausages and quick lunches are also sold.

Uruguayans strolling along the observation deck in Punta del Este.

VACATION TIME

During the summer (December to March), most Uruguayans living in or near Montevideo will spend weekends and holidays at one of the many beaches strung out along the drive from the capital to Punta del Este. Those keeping an eye on expenses will either go for just a day or will look for economical cottages to rent. Those with more money to spend have villas or can afford to rent homes in Punta del Este for the two-month summer vacation. Wherever vacationers end up, however, summertime will be family barbecue time. Every rental house and villa has its own outdoor wood-fired barbecue, and the most popular summer food is grilled meat.

PUNTA DEL ESTE Punta del Este is the main tourist resort in Uruguay. When it is open during the summer, it is the place to be. Located to the east of Montevideo, Punta del Este has a 25-mile (40-km) stretch of beach. Its beauty is comparable to the fabled resort areas of the French Riviera. Throughout the season, there are many sport competitions there and activities for singles and families. It is as if the cultural heartbeat of Uruguay shifts for the summer season from Montevideo to Punta del Este. There are open-air concerts, theatrical performances and premieres, dance performances, and recitals that are held at the two big clubs: Club del Lago and the Cantegril.

There are also local-level sport competitions and beauty contests. The seashore season ends with the Festival of the Sea. After that, everyone packs up and goes home for another 10 months of life in the city.

PIRIAPOLIS Piriapolis, also to the east of Montevideo, was Uruguay's first seaside resort. It was founded in 1893 by Francisco Piria, who built the mellow landmark Argentino Hotel there. Piriapolis is still an active resort town, but it is much quieter than Punta del Este. It attracts people who want a more restful vacation than the wild nights Punta del Este provides. Recently, thermal baths using heated ocean water have opened. People now visit Piriapolis especially for the health and beauty spas.

A crowded beach at Punta del Este, overlooked by substantial high-rise buildings.

OTHER DESTINATIONS Uruguayans who prefer something different can venture to the interior of the country for a vacation. Some popular destinations include the thermal springs near Salto and Paysandú in the northwest. The springs there result from warm water bubbling up to the surface, creating inviting pools. Family resorts have been built around the springs, with hotels, movie theaters, shopping areas, and restaurants.

For those interested in nature, there is Rocha department in the southeast. There the coast is much rockier and, being on the Atlantic Ocean, the water is rougher. Small fishing villages are scattered along the coast, and the shore rocks support a large colony of sea lions. Fishing enthusiasts find boats for hire, and nature lovers enjoy the wild feeling of the remote Rocha seacoast. Inland, there are parks and nature reserves that are home to Uruguay's wildlife. Some of those beautiful parks permit hunting and fishing, while others are for observation only.

Motorists also enjoy taking country drives throughout the year to see the fantastic scenery of the plains. Some of the old ranch houses are open for guests as bed-and-breakfast inns—new life for classic estancias.

FESTIVALS

Folk musicians playing *bombo legueros*, traditional drums, at Plaza Constitución, Montevideo, during a festival.

≫**U**RUGUAY CELEBRATES BOTH religious holidays and secular ones drawn from its history.

EPIPHANY

In many Roman Catholic countries Epiphany is as important as Christmas because it is the day when the Three Kings, or the Three Wise Men, visited Jesus and gave him gifts. In Uruguay, Epiphany has become an African-Uruguayan celebration. Black slaves generally were close to the white people for whom they worked during the colonial period. As a result, they easily converted to Catholicism and celebrated Epiphany as the day when the black king, Balthazar, visited Jesus. As one of the Three Kings, or Wise Men, Balthazar was later made a saint.

Entertainers performing a traditional dance.

Uruguayans are not very religious. For that reason, some of the traditional Christian celebrations have different, nonreligious, names. For example, Easter Week is called Semana Criolla, or Tourism Week, and Christmas is Family Day. Many of the other public holidays are celebrations of important moments in Uruguayan history.

January 1	*New Year's Day*
January 6	*Epiphany, Day of Saint Balthazar*
February/March	*Carnival (Mardi Gras)*
March/April	*Semana Criolla, or Tourism Week (Easter Week)*
March/April	*Fiesta del Mar, or Festival of the Sea*
April 19	*Landing of the Oriental 33*
May 1	*Labor Day*
May 18	*Day of the Battle of Las Piedras*
June 19	*Birthday of General Artigas*
July 18	*Constitution Day*
August 25	*Independence Day*
October 12	*Discovery of America (Columbus Day), also known as Día de la Raza or Day of Race*
November 2	*All Souls' Day*
December 8	*Beach Day*
December 25	*Family Day (Christmas)*

Most blacks lived in Montevideo throughout the colonial period and into the 19th century. At that time they organized themselves into groups called nations, based on their areas of origin in Africa. Those black nations were mutual-aid societies, meaning that members helped each other in times of need. Each nation also sponsored its own dance and parade group. Periodically through the year, the nations would organize dance celebrations known as a *candombes*. Each nation elected a king and queen for every *candombe*; then they would compete with other kings and queens to be judged the best dancers.

On Epiphany, African Uruguayans of Montevideo today organize an exceptionally large *candombe* celebration. The nations parade throughout the city, each playing its own music and dancing in their group's competitions.

CARNIVAL

Carnival is linked to the Roman Catholic observation of Lent, the 40-day period before Easter when practicing Catholics give up eating meat to show compassion at the death of Christ on Good Friday. Carnival takes place three days to a week before Lent begins and is similar to Mardi Gras in New Orleans. It is everyone's last chance to feast, eat meat, and celebrate before the serious time of Lent begins.

Carnival has been celebrated in Europe since the Middle Ages. The name comes from the Latin *carne vale*, which means "farewell to meat." Carnival

Participants in the street theater called *tablado.*

has a long tradition in the New World and has been celebrated in Montevideo since the earliest colonial times.

The modern Carnival in Uruguay lasts three days, during which there are parades of dancers and decorated floats moving through the streets. The African-Uruguayan community is famous for the dance groups it sends to the colorful processions. A Queen of Carnival is elected as the most beautiful girl in Montevideo. Two vice-queens make up her court. There are light shows in the streets and an atmosphere of general gaiety.

One distinctive feature of the Montevideo Carnival is the street theater or *tablado*. *Tablados* refer to makeshift stages where *murgas* can showcase the performance that they have been practicing for Carnival. *Murgas* and other carnival groups are invited to perform at various street theaters, or at the Teatro de Verano (summer theater), a big outdoor amphitheater where *murga* contests are held. Townspeople build huge stages on street corners and hire writers and directors to create plays in which the local people will

Parque Rodó, the main public park in Montevideo, is the scene of all the highlights of Carnival, including dance groups, street theater, and special music.

Young boys dressed up for Carnival merrymaking.

act. Different communities compete earnestly with one another to put on the best *tablado* and will spend a lot of money to make their play the most spectacular with lights and set decorations. The plays are usually pure fantasy or romance, but sometimes they make fun of local politicians or international celebrities. Musicians also create special songs for the *tablados murgas*. They often have a political or witty observation in the lyrics.

Although Carnival officially lasts three days, the dancers and theater groups continue to perform in public parks and hotels for as long as a month. So much planning, cost, and preparation are involved in these productions that the organizers and actors want everyone to be able to enjoy their creative efforts longer than the official holiday calls for.

SEMANA CRIOLLA, OR TOURISM WEEK

In place of the religious celebrations of Easter, Uruguayans prefer to remember their own cultural past. Semana Criolla, or Creole Week, is named in remembrance of the first descendants of Europeans born in the New

A gaucho leaps from one horse to another during a Semana Criolla competition.

World, called creoles, or *criollos* (kree-OHL-yohs) in Spanish. The main motif of the week is to recall and celebrate the gauchos. Men wear typical gaucho clothing and paraphernalia take part in various contests of gaucho skills, including riding bulls, breaking broncos, and trick riding.

Only 30 men are allowed to compete, and they are carefully chosen among applicants from all over the country. Winners take prizes for the best costume, riding equipment, dancing, singing, lassoing, and bronco busting. Women also compete; Uruguayans still remember a woman competitor named Nieves Mira who was very beautiful and talented. Another famous gaucho was El Fantasma, or The Ghost. He was an African Uruguayan who did all his trick riding with his poncho covering his eyes!

The gaucho events are quite spectacular and many tourists pour into Montevideo to see the competitions. That is why Semana Criolla is also sometimes called Tourism Week.

BEACH DAY

Uruguay is south of the equator, so the seasons are reversed. December 8 is the official opening of the beaches and the beginning of the summer vacation period for Uruguayans. Before anyone steps into the ocean, a priest blesses the waters to make them safe. There are also regattas, or sailing races, at various ports. In Carrasco there is an international shooting competition.

FIESTA DEL MAR, OR FESTIVAL OF THE SEA

The very popular Fiesta del Mar takes place at the end of the southern hemisphere's summer, around March or April. At night the beach between Punta del Este and Punta Ballena is brightly lit with lights. The first part of the celebration is a parade of colorfully decorated boats. Later, a Queen of the Sea is crowned at one of the social clubs on the beach.

Contestants for the coveted royal title wait on the shore for a swimmer dressed as Neptune, the Roman sea god, to emerge from the water. He will approach the winner and place a crown on her head. The Queen will then be paraded through Punta del Este, with a long train of cars following her float. The celebration ends with an hour-long fireworks display, officially ending the summer as well.

HISTORICAL HOLIDAYS

The most important of the national holidays is Independence Day, on August 25, when ceremonies are held in Independence Square in Montevideo. Constitution Day, on July 18, celebrates the first constitution drafted and signed in 1830. Finally, April 19 is the day when everyone remembers the 1823 landing in Montevideo of the Oriental 33—a group of revolutionaries led by Juan Antonio Lavalleja—striving to free Uruguay from the Brazilians. All of these historic days are public holidays and occasions to display heartfelt patriotism.

Two days are devoted to the memory of General José Artigas. One is on June 19, which commemorates his birthday. The other is May 18, which celebrates his famous victory at the Battle of Las Piedras. Las Piedras is a village not far from Montevideo where, in 1811, Artigas and his small band of soldiers confronted Spanish loyalists. After six hours of combat, Artigas emerged victorious.

The battle is not significant because of the number of Spanish losses or the scale of the victory but because its triumph gave people hope that the Spaniards could be beaten. As a result of his victory, Artigas was able to rally a large force of men when he marched out of Montevideo. That event made Artigas famous as "the chief of the Orientals," as Uruguayans were called at the time.

In 2007 President Tabaré Vázquez implemented Día del Nunca Más (Day of Never Again). Día del Nunca Más falls on the birthday of General José Artigas, June 19, but does not have anything to do with Artigas. Instead, Día del Nunca Más is a day of remembrance of the atrocities that occurred during the dictatorship and the period leading up to it. It is a day whereby Uruguay asserts that state terrorism and guerrilla warfare will never again be allowed to take place.

Politicians and other important citizens deliver ceremonious speeches on Independence Day extolling the courageous struggles for independence— waged first against the Spanish and then against the Brazilians.

NVIOS A DOMICILIO ☏ 410

FOOD

Fruits and vegetables displayed
at a store in Montevideo.

U RUGUAYAN CUISINE IS THE RESULT of many influences, including gaucho, Spanish, and Italian. When all those traditions are combined, the result is delicious.

TYPICAL FOODS AND BEVERAGES

The central dish in all main meals in Uruguay is meat. In the early days of independence and trade with Britain, the main export was not meat but hides for English leather industries. That was because there was no

People enjoying a meal outdoors at a restaurant in Colonia.

The influence of other cultures in Uruguayan cuisine can be found in the way Uruguayans cook their food as well as in the things that they eat. Meat is an essential part of the Uruguayan diet, and the favored method of cooking is the barbeque. A typical meal would feature meat as the main dish and potatoes, salad, and bread as sides. The most popular drink in Uruguay is maté.

The *parillada*, or barbecue, is very popular in Uruguay.

easy way to ship fresh meat in the years before refrigeration. When gauchos rounded up animals for slaughter, they were left with literally tons of meat once the hides were removed. Meat thus became the heartbeat of the Uruguayan diet. Late in the 19th century canning technology was developed, and meat could then be exported to Europe.

The barbecue or *parillada* (pah-ree-YAH-dah) is the most popular way to cook meat. All Uruguayan homes have an outdoor grill for that purpose. They burn wood or wood charcoal to cook with rather than gas because it gives the meat a more desirable flavor. Meat is also processed into other forms. A favorite is *moncilla* (mone-SEE-yah), a blood sausage. Meat may also be used in *empanadas* (aym-pah-NAH-dahs), sweet or savory pastry turnovers. *Chivitos* (chee-VEE-tohs) are a kind of local fast-food sandwich that usually includes egg, tomato, thinly sliced steak, cheese, and lettuce piled high in a bun. Other fast foods using meat are *olímpicos* (oh-LEEM-pee-kohs), *húngaros* (OON-gah-rohs), and *panchos* (PAHN-chohs, hot dogs). *Olímpicos* are essentially club sandwiches. *Húngaros* and *panchos* are both sausages served on buns like hot dogs, but *húngaros* are very spicy. A country favorite is meat stew or *estofado* (ay-stoh-FAH-doh). That gaucho favorite originated on the open plains and is very hearty.

A typical family meal includes meat as the main dish (usually beef or chicken) with potatoes, bread, and a green salad or cooked vegetables. Potatoes are the essential accompaniment to huge slabs of steak.

With the large numbers of Italian immigrants arriving in the late 19th and early 20th century, Uruguay's diet was supplemented with other foods. Some of the first businesses opened by Italians were pasta-making factories. They also imported their favorite foods such as Parmesan cheese and prosciutto (dry-cured Italian ham). As those became popular in pasta and pizza dishes, Uruguayans began producing their own. Typical Italian-Uruguayan pizza is made in a wood-burning oven in keeping with the barbecue tradition.

The Spanish heritage can be seen in the way seafood and stews are cooked. Many local dishes feature mussels, shrimps, and cockles as well as freshwater and saltwater fish. Along the seacoast, restaurants offer freshly caught fish and shellfish.

Desserts also have been influenced by Uruguay's European heritage. Pastry was introduced by the Italian immigrants, and most cafés feature delicious examples. The Spanish influence on desserts is seen in the frequent use of *dulce de leche* (DOOL-say day LAY-chay, literally sweetness of milk), a kind of thick, concentrated sweetened milk. *Dulce* is used as a sauce with fruit or spread on bread and pastry. It is incredibly sweet and rich.

Most Uruguayans today do the bulk of their grocery shopping at a supermarket. Before large supermarkets became common, people bought their food from shops specializing in particular products. If they wanted the freshest vegetables, they went to the greengrocer, for meat they visited their local butcher, for fish the fishmonger, and so on. The reason for shopping that way was that most working-class and middle-class people did not have the space or appliances to store food for a long time. They could not freeze food for later use, so they did their shopping every day or every few days. Those specialized stores, however, are no longer as prominent as they once were.

Specialty shops have lost prominence, with people now preferring to shop at supermarkets.

The drink of choice throughout the day is maté, a tea made with the leaves of the yerba maté, which is native to South America. Europeans learned to drink maté from the indigenous peoples. Maté has quite a bit of caffeine and is used a little like coffee in North American culture. Uruguayans drink so much maté, many of them carry a thermos of hot water and a supply of dried leaves everywhere they go so they can prepare fresh cups of the beverage on the spot.

Uruguay produces its own beer and wine. One particularly Uruguayan drink is *clericó* (klay-ree-KOH), which is a mixture of white wine and fruit juice. Sparkling wine mixed with white wine is called *medio y medio* (MAY-dee-oh ee MAY-dee-oh) or "half and half."

MEALTIMES

The Uruguayan pattern of eating is similar to that found in southern Europe. Breakfast for many Uruguayans is a cup of coffee or maté and a large croissant. Working people usually return home for a long lunch break, often lasting from 12 or 1 P.M. to 3 or 4 P.M.

MATÉ

Yerba maté is a relative of the European holly tree. Its leaves are harvested and dried. To make maté, pack a cup—usually a maté gourd—full of the leaves and then add hot water. The mixture is left to steep. When the water is infused with the flavor of the maté, the straw, or bombilla, is dipped into the container full of soaked leaves, and the warm liquid is sipped through it. Maté is an acquired taste—it is fairly bitter and has an earthy flavor.

Social relevance is attached to maté drinking. Among indigenous peoples, maté drinking was done in small groups, with the cup passed around for everyone to sip. The first Europeans to adopt this social habit were the gauchos who gathered together in small groups around the campfire in the evenings. Not only do people like to drink it all day but, as often as possible, they gather together to share the drink.

Interestingly, during the military dictatorship, when most forms of public meeting were prohibited, maté gatherings remained one of the few ways people could meet legally and talk with one another. Those wanting to pass along information, or simply to be together in social groups, gathered at local maté snack shops. Since there was nothing noticeably political about the practice, the police and army ignored it.

Lunch is the main meal of the day. It usually includes a first course such as a salad or soup, a main course of meat and vegetables, and dessert. Since lunch is the heaviest meal of the day, people often take a nap afterward to help with digestion; they then return to work until 7 or 8 P.M. Later in the evening they will have another, lighter meal. Their supper may not be eaten until 10 or 11 at night, which is not very late since they took a nap at midday. The relaxed cultural usage of taking naps is, however, becoming a thing of the past as demanding work schedules now do not allow most Uruguayans to lie down for a while in the afternoon.

EATING OUT

Eating out is very popular in the cities. Montevideo offers every type of restaurant and price range imaginable, and restaurants are open morning, noon, and night. In the mornings, cafés everywhere serve coffee and light breakfasts for people on their way to work.

At midmorning, many workers take a short break from work and gather in cafeterias for some maté or coffee and a chat with coworkers. These corner snack bars are great for mixing all types of people. It is not unusual for blue-collar workers, secretaries, students, and businesspeople to go to the same snack bar.

People who cannot return home for lunch will eat at a restaurant near their workplace or school. Many restaurants cater to those eating out with something called the fixed, three-course menu of the day—a set meal that does not allow customers to choose what they want. The advantage for the restaurant is that there is no need to stock and prepare many different foods; for the thrifty customer, the fixed-price menu is fairly cheap. People often have a favorite place to eat lunch and go there every day.

For the late evening meal, there are a variety of foods and styles of service in Montevideo and other big cities. From Italian gourmet to pizza parlors, from pubs to fancy French restaurants—the diners can take their pick. The most popular type of restaurant, called a *parrillada* (barbecue, or grill), caters to the Uruguayan passion for grilled meat and uses only wood charcoal.

In recent years, health-aware North Americans have been eating less red meat and smaller portions. Not so for the Uruguayans, who continue to appreciate one-pound cuts on their plates.

Another specialty restaurant is the gaucho club. The busy clubs are decorated with pictures and mementos of gaucho life. They specialize in gaucho dishes such as *asado con cuero*—large pieces of beef grilled with the hide left on—and *mazamorra* (mah-zah-MOHR-rah), ground corn with milk. For simpler tastes, there are *cervecerías* (sayr-vay-say-REE-ahs) or beer gardens. Along with beer, they serve *chivitos*—the super large steak sandwich—and other snack foods. But do not even think about eating until at least 10 at night or you might find that none of the restaurants have opened yet.

Away from the largest cities, there are few fancy restaurants and certainly no foreign food. In rural areas, distances are much greater and budgets much tighter, so country people rarely tend to eat out. The core of their diet is still meat and potatoes. Another rural staple is rice, often used as an inexpensive and nutritious filler in soups and stews. Uruguay is an important exporter of rice. People in the countryside eat less fish, being farther from the coast and its bountiful catches.

Uruguay set a world record in the *Libro Guiness* in 2008, hosting the largest *asado* (barbecue). In all, 26,455 pounds (12,000 kg) of chopped meat were grilled by 1,252 cooks on 4,921 feet (1,500 m) of grills. According to the organizers, Uruguayan cattle are grass fed and free from antibiotics and hormones, and therefore are tastier and healthier.

Uruguayans in the city tend to eat out far more than their rural counterparts.

ALBONDIAGAS (MEATBALL STEW)

Meatballs:

5 tablespoons (75 ml) vegetable oil (divided)

1 onion, finely chopped

1 tomato, peeled and chopped

1 teaspoon (5 ml) sugar

Salt, pepper, hot ground pepper to taste

1 pound veal (450 g), finely ground

1 cup (250 ml) fresh breadcrumbs

4 tablespoons (60 ml) Parmesan cheese, grated

¼ cup (110 g) seedless raisins

¼ teaspoon (1 ml) nutmeg, grated or ground

2 eggs, beaten

Small amount of milk if needed

1 tablespoon (15 ml) flour

Broth:

1 tablespoon (15 ml) vegetable oil

1 onion, finely chopped

1½ cups (375 ml) beef stock

1½ cups (375 ml) dry red wine (optional)

¼ teaspoon (1 ml) thyme

¼ teaspoon (1 ml) oregano

1 bay leaf

Salt and pepper to taste

Additional stock and wine, if necessary

Yield: 4—6 servings

Heat 2 tablespoons (30 ml) of oil in a skillet. Sauté the onions until soft. Add tomato, hot pepper, sugar, salt and pepper. Cook, stirring from time to time, until the mixture is thick and fairly dry. Let the mixture cool. Mix the veal, breadcrumbs, Parmesan cheese, raisins, nutmeg, and tomato mixture in a bowl. Add the beaten eggs and mix thoroughly. Add a splash of milk if the mixture is too dry to hold together. Form into balls about 2 inches (5 cm) in diameter and flour them lightly. Heat the remaining 3 tablespoons (45 ml) of oil in the skillet and sauté the meatballs until lightly browned. Lift them out and set aside when done.

To make the broth, heat one tablespoon (15 ml) of oil in a saucepan and sauté the onions until very soft. Add the beef stock, wine, thyme, oregano, and bay leaf. Simmer for a few minutes to blend the flavors. Season with salt and pepper to taste. Add meatballs, cover and cook for about 30 minutes over low heat until done. Add more stock and wine in equal amounts if more gravy is needed. Serve meatballs with rice or any starchy vegetables, using the broth as gravy.

FLOATING ISLAND MERINGUE

3 or 4 large egg yolks

¼ cup (60 ml) sugar

Pinch of salt

2 cups (500 ml) milk

1 teaspoon (5 ml) vanilla, rum, or sherry, or the
   grated zest of 1 lemon

3 egg whites

pinch of salt

3 tablespoons (45 ml) sugar

½ teaspoon (2.5 ml) vanilla, or a few drops of
   almond extract

Yield: 4 servings

Preparation of the custard sauce:

Beat slightly the 3 or 4 egg yolks. Add ¼ cup (60 ml) sugar and a pinch of salt. Scald the 2 cups (500 ml) of milk and slowly stir it into the egg mixture. Place the custard over a very low fire. Stir it constantly until it just begins to thicken. Take care that it does not boil. Alternatively, stir over simmering water until it thickens slightly. Strain and cool the custard. Fold in 1 teaspoon (5 ml) vanilla, rum, or sherry, or a little grated lemon zest. Place the custard sauce in a baking dish and chill it thoroughly. The custard will not be firm.

Preparation of the Floating Island:

Whip the egg whites and a pinch of salt until stiff peaks are formed. Still whipping constantly, very slowly add 3 tablespoons (45 ml) sugar and ½ teaspoon (2.5 ml) vanilla or a few drops of almond extract. Using a large spoon, heap the stiff egg whites gently on top of the custard sauce. Place the dish in a 500°F (260°C) oven for 2 minutes, until the tips of the meringue are light brown, or place under a broiler until the tips brown. Serve it hot or cold, with fruit if desired.

A   **B**   **C**   **D**

- Capital city
- Major town
- ▲ Mountain peak

Feet		Meters
16,500		5,000
9,900		3,000
6,600		2,000
3,300		1,000
1,650		500
660		200
0		0

1

2

3

4

Río Cuareim

ARTIGAS

Cuchilla de Belén

Rivera

BRAZIL

Salto Grande

Salto

SALTO

Cuchilla de Haedo

Tacuarembó

RIVERA

ARGENTINA

PAYSANDÚ

TACUAREMBÓ

Río Negro

Paysandú

Río Uruguay

Melo

CERRO LARGO

RÍO NEGRO

Black River Lake

Merín Lagoon

Fray Bentos

Río Negro (Black River)

DURAZNO

Río Yí

TREINTA Y TRES

Mercedes

Río Yí

Grande

SORIANO

FLORES

FLORIDA

Cuchilla

LAVALLEJA

ROCHA

COLONIA

SAN JOSÉ

Río Santa Lucía

Minas

Mt. Catedral (1,684ft / 513m) ▲

Colonia

Canelones

MALDONADO

Buenos Aires

CANELONES

Las Piedras

▲ Mt. Animas

MONTEVIDEO

Piriapolis

Isla de Lobos

Punta del Este

ATLANTIC

OCEAN

N

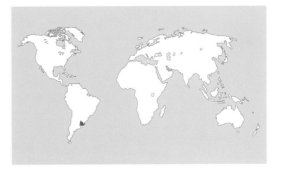

ECONOMIC URUGUAY

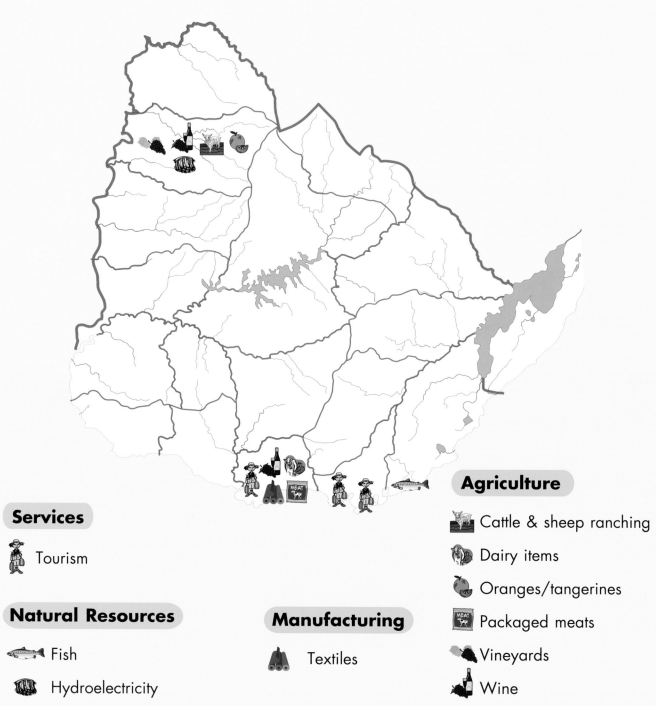

Services

Tourism

Natural Resources

Fish

Hydroelectricity

Manufacturing

Textiles

Agriculture

Cattle & sheep ranching

Dairy items

Oranges/tangerines

Packaged meats

Vineyards

Wine

ABOUT THE ECONOMY

OVERVIEW

Uruguay has a middle-income economy that depends on agriculture, a well-educated workforce, and high levels of social spending. The state is deeply involved in the economy, owning either fully or partially companies in infrastructure, finance, telecommunication, and transportation. An increase in the agriculture and agro industry helped Uruguay surge forward in economic growth from 6.6 percent to 7.4 percent (2007) in two years. The investment climate is generally positive, thus the remittance of capital and profits for foreign companies remains unrestricted. Uruguay has been developing the commercial uses of technology, becoming the first exporter of software in Latin America. There is a huge inflow of foreign investment to the tourism industry and also in the recruitment, training, and deployment of foreign workers.

GROSS DOMESTIC PRODUCT (GDP)
$42.46 billion (2008 estimate)

GDP GROWTH
8.5 percent (2008 estimate)

INFLATION RATE
9.2 percent (2008)

CURRENCY
Uruguay peso (UYU peso)
1 U.S. dollar = 24.5 UYU pesos (2009)

NATURAL RESOURCES
Arable land, pastures, hydroelectric power, granite, marble, and fisheries

AGRICULTURAL PRODUCTS
Rice, wheat, soybeans, barley, livestock (cattle, sheep), fish, and forestry

INDUSTRY
Food processing, electrical machinery, transportation equipment, petroleum products, wool, textiles, leather apparel, chemicals, beverages, and tobacco

MAJOR EXPORTS
Meat, hides, leather, wool, wool products, fish, rice, and furs

MAJOR IMPORTS
Machinery, chemicals, fuel, vehicles, paper, and plastic

EXPORT PARTNERS
United States, Brazil, Argentina, Mexico, Germany, China, and Russia

IMPORT PARTNERS
Brazil, Argentina, United States, China, Venezuela, Paraguay, Nigeria

POPULATION BELOW POVERTY LINE
27.4 percent (2006)

WORKFORCE
1.641 million (2008 estimate)

UNEMPLOYMENT RATE
7.6 percent (2008 estimate)

CULTURAL URUGUAY

Arapey Springs
Arapey Springs is one of the oldest hot spring resorts in Uruguay. It is located about 50 miles (80 km) north of the city of Salto. It is a popular tourist spot and many visit the springs for relaxation and also for the waters' reputed medicinal and healing properties.

Museo de la Revolución Industrial
This old abandoned meat factory was one of Uruguay's most important industrial complexes, producing meat products that were once a staple all over the world. Visitors can take a walk through passageways and view slaughterhouses located just behind the museum.

The Historical Borough/ Cultural Heritage of Humanity
In 1995, UNESCO declared the Historical Borough of Colonia del Sacramento the "Culture Heritage of Humanity." History can be found everywhere in this area, from its cobbled streets to drawbridges, all testament of Uruguay's colonial past.

Casa Pueblo
Casa Pueblo is an art museum situated in Punta del Este. The art museum not only houses work by renowned artist Carlos Paéz Vilario, but was designed by him.

Ciudad Vieja
Ciudad Vieja (old city) is the oldest part of Montevideo. Many buildings with beautiful architecture dating back to Uruguay's colonial era can be found here. The Old City now boasts an electric nightlife and many pubs and clubs are found in this district.

Gaucho Museum
The Gaucho Museum is housed in the oldest house in Montevideo. Snippets and glimpses of the revered gaucho life (such as clothes and tools) are on display, along with gaucho artwork.

Carnival Museum
Carnival is one of the most celebrated and anticipated festivals in Uruguay. This museum showcases not only beautiful costumes used during Carnival over the years, but also the work that goes into preparing for this extravagant festival. Visitors are also able to appreciate the different cultures that have influenced Carnival.

Lemanja
On February 2 every year, devotees of the goddess of the sea, Lemanja, gather at the beaches at Montevideo and Punta del Este to present offerings and to receive her blessings.

ABOUT THE CULTURE

OFFICIAL NAME
Oriental Republic of Uruguay

FLAG DESCRIPTION
The flag of Uruguay has a field of nine equal horizontal stripes of white alternating with blue. The stripes represent the nine original counties. A yellow sun, depicting a human face known as the Sun of May, is located in a white square in the upper hoist-side corner. Sixteen sun rays, alternating between triangular and wavy, burst forth from the sun.

CAPITAL
Montevideo

POPULATION
3,494,382 million (2009 estimate)

BIRTHRATE
14.17 births per 1,000 population (2008 estimate)

DEATH RATE
9.12 deaths per 1,000 population (2008 estimate)

AGE DISTRIBUTION
Under 15: 22.7 percent; 15—64: 64 percent; 65 and over: 13.3 percent (2008 estimate)

ETHNIC GROUPS
Spanish or Italian 88 percent; mestizo 8 percent; African 4 percent

RELIGIOUS GROUPS
Roman Catholic 47.1 percent; Protestant 11.1 percent; nonaffiliated 23.2 percent; Jewish 0.3 percent; nonprofessing or others 18.3 percent

MAIN LANGUAGES
Spanish, Portuñol, also called Fronterizo or Bayano, (Portuguese-Spanish mix on the Uruayan-Brazilian frontier)

LITERACY RATE
98 percent

IMPORTANT HOLIDAYS
January 1: New Year's Day; February, March*: Carnival; March, April*: Good Friday and Easter; April 20: Landing of the Oriental 33 Patriots; May 18: Battle of Las Piedras; June 19: Birth of General José G. Artigas, and Día del Nunca Mas; July 18: Constitution Day; August 25: National Independence Day; October 12: Día de la Raza
*movable dates

TIME LINE

IN URUGUAY	IN THE WORLD
6000 B.C. Human settlement in area now known as Uruguay	**323 B.C.** Alexander the Great's empire stretches from Greece to India.
	1206–1368 Genghis Khan unifies the Mongols and starts conquest of the world. At its height, the Mongol Empire under Kublai Khan stretches from China to Persia and parts of Europe and Russia.
1680 Portuguese found Colonia del Sacramento (Uruguay)	
1726 Montevideo is founded.	
1750 The first African slaves arrive in Montevideo.	**1775–83** The American Revolution
1799 José Gervasio Artigas is appointed head of Montevideo militia.	**1789–99** The French Revolution
1811 General José G. Artigas launches a successful revolt against Spain, the Exodus of the Orientals.	
1825 Uruguay declares its independence from Brazil and adheres to a regional federation with Argentina.	
1828 Uruguay becomes an independent state.	
1830 Uruguay's first constitution is adopted. General José Frutuoso Riveria becomes president.	
1865–70 War of the Triple Alliance (Argentina, Brazil, and Uruguay aligned against Paraguay).	

IN URUGUAY	IN THE WORLD
1903–07 José Batlle y Ordóñez is elected president.	
	1914 World War I begins.
1911–15 José Batlle y Ordóñez reelected president and initiates Batllismo reforms.	
1930 The first soccer World Cup is held in Montevideo. Uruguay wins.	**1939** World War II begins.
	1945 The United States drops atomic bombs on Hiroshima and Nagasaki.
1973 Armed forces depose democratic government and establish a brutal dictatorship.	
1984 The military regime falls.	**1986** Nuclear power disaster at Chernobyl in Ukraine.
1991 Uruguay becomes a founding member of MERCOSUR	
1994 Former president Julio María Sanguinetti of the Colorado Party wins a new term.	**1997** Hong Kong is returned to China.
2001 Financial crisis impels up to 15 percent of Uruguay's population to leave the country in search of work.	**2003** War in Iraq begins.
2004 Dr. Tabaré Vázquez wins the presidency.	**2004** Indian Ocean earthquake and tsunami.
2006 Uruguay pays off its billion-dollar debt to the International Monetary Fund.	
2007 Argentineans cross border into Uruguay to protest at a paper pulp mill.	
2008 President Tabaré Ramón Vázquez Rosas announces discovery of natural gas field off Uruguay's Atlantic coast.	**2008** Earthquake in Sichuan, China, kills nearly 15,000. Terrorists kill at least 150 in Mumbai, India.

GLOSSARY

Batllismo (bahj-JEES-moh)
Government and social reform designed by José Batlle at the beginning of the 20th century.

bombilla (bohm-BEE-ya)
Straw, usually silver, used to sip maté.

candombe (can-DOHM-bay)
Music and dance of African-Uruguayan origin.

Cocoliche (ko-ko-LEE-chay)
A Spanish-Italian dialect spoken by first-generation Italian immigrants in Buenos Aires and Montevideo.

criollos (kree-OHL-yohs)
Creoles, the first people of European descent born in the New World.

estancia
Large ranch.

Fronterizo (fron-tayr-EE-zoh)
Dialect (also called Portuñol and Bayano) that is a mix of Spanish and Portuguese spoken on the Brazilian-Uruguayan border.

Garra Charrúa (GAR-rah char-ROO-ah)
(Charrúan talon) Expression meaning brave, persistent, and fierce.

gaucho
Traditional cowboy of the southern regions of South America.

Lunfardo (loon-FAR-doh)
Working-class slang used in Buenos Aires and Montevideo.

maté
Herbal steeped beverage made with dried yerba maté leaves.

MERCOSUR (Southern Cone Common Market)
The 1991 free trade agreement between Uruguay, Paraguay, Brazil, and Argentina.

mestizo
Person of mixed Spanish and Indian blood.

murga (MOOR-gah)
Carnival music group and their songs.

Porteño (por-TAYN-yoh)
A variety of Spanish spoken in Buenos Aires and Montevideo.

rastra (RAHS-trah)
Wide belt made of leather and metal worn by gauchos.

tablado (tah-BLAH-doh)
Neighborhood street theater performed during Carnival.

Tupamaros (too-pah-MAR-ohs
Guerrilla fighters who challenged the government before the military dictatorship.

yerba maté
Plant whose dried leaves are used to steep the Uruguayan tealike drink called maté.

FOR FURTHER INFORMATION

BOOKS

Clark, Gregor. *Uruguay*. (Lonely Planet Custom Guide). Oakland, CA: Lonely Planet, 2008.

Shields, Charles. *Uruguay* (South America Today). Broomall, PA: Mason Crest Publishers, 2009.

WEBSITES

Amber Waves. www.ers.usda.gov/AmberWaves/April08/Features/GlobalMarket.htm

BBC News. Timeline: Uruguay. http://news.bbc.co.uk/2/hi/americas/1229362.stm

CIA World Factbook. www.cia.gov/cia/publications/factbook/index.html

This is Uruguay. http://guay.wordpress.com

Timeline Uruguay. http://timelines.ws/countries/URUGUAY.HTML

Travel Document Systems. www.traveldocs.com/uy/economy.htm

U.S. Department of State. www.state.gov/r/pa/ei/bgn/2091.htm

Voyages. www.alvoyages.com/articles/south-america/uruguay.html

MUSIC CD

Jaime Roos. *Candombe, Murga y Rocanrol*. Sony Music, 2004.

Los Olimarenos. *Mis 30 Mejores Canciones*. Sony BMG Europe, 2007.

FILM

El Baño del Papa. Directed by César Charlone and Enrique Fernández. Film Movement, 2007.

BIBLIOGRAPHY

Buckman, Robert T. *Latin America*. The World Today Series. Harpers Ferry, WV: Stryker-Post Publications, 1997.

Clark, George. *Uruguay*. Lonely Planet Custom Guide. Oakland, CA: Lonely Planet, 2008.

Coatsworth, Elizabeth (editor). *Tales of the Gauchos: Stories by W.H. Hudson*. New York: Alfred A. Knopf, 1946.

Fisher, John R. *Latin America: From Conquest to Independence*. London: Rupert Hart-Davis, 1971.

Hudson, Rex A., and Sandra W. Meditz (editors). *Uruguay: A Country Study*. Area Handbook Series. Washington, DC: Federal Research Division, Library of Congress, 1992.

McNaspy, C. J. *Lost Cities of Paraguay: Art and Architecture of the Jesuit Reductions, 1607—1767*. Chicago: Loyola University Press, 1982.

_____. *Minnesota-Uruguay*., Minneapolis, MN: Partners of the Americas, 2008.

Morrison, Marion. *Let's Visit Uruguay*. Bridgeport, CT: Burke Publishing, 1985.

Sosnowski, S., and L. B. Popkin (editors). *Repression, Exile and Democracy: Uruguayan Culture*. Series: Latin America in Translation. Durham, NC: Duke University Press, 1993.

Tames, Richard. *The Conquest of South America*. London: Methuen, 1974.

Wilbert, Johannes, and Karin Simoneau. *Folk Literature of the Makka Indians*. Los Angeles: UCLA Latin American Center Publications, 1991.

INDEX

INDEX

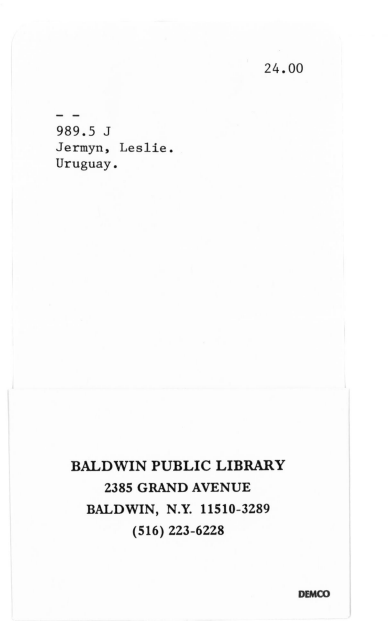

24.00

DEMCO